BARBECUES AND PICNICS

Better Homes and Gardens

MEREDITH PRESS

BETTER HOMES AND GARDENS CREATIVE COOKING LIBRARY, SIXTH PRINTING

Contents

Barbecues easy and elegant....... 6

Fancy franks, burgers
Bargains to barbecue
Birds in blue-ribbon ways
Fishermen's favorites
Company meats
Over-the-coals kabobs
Grill-side salads, vegetables,
    and breads
Easy outdoor desserts
Extra-special extras—
    appetizers and relishes

Real cool cooking............. 38

Patio sandwich suppers
Salad-plate refreshers
Have a porch picnic

Meals on the go!.............. 50

Cook-a-little picnics
Spread-out-and-serve basket lunches
Eat lunch hobo style

This seal means recipe goodness!

Every recipe in this book is *endorsed* by Better Homes and Gardens Test Kitchen. Each food was tested over and over till it rated superior —in practicality, ease of preparation, and deliciousness.

← One winner among many—
Rotisserie Turkey rates a final fillip
of flavor from smoking hickory

Hilo Franks and pineapple slices sizzle and glaze to a tart-sweet finish,

Barbecues easy and elegant

Hawaiian as a hula.

Whether you're feasting with
family or friends, take your
choice of bargains or company cuts.
They all are sure to please.
Page ahead to fancy franks and
burgers, bargains to barbecue, birds
in blue-ribbon ways, fishermen's
favorites and company meats.

Also, over-the-coals kabobs,
grill-side salads, vegetables, and
breads, easy outdoor desserts,
extra-special extras — appetizers
and relishes. Barbecues are such
delicious fun — plan one soon!

Fancy franks, burgers

....

Island Treat

Honeydew Balls with Lime Wedges
Hilo Franks with
Grilled Pineapple Slices
Crisp Green Salad with
Orange Dressing*
Toasted Buttered Bun Halves
Hot Banana Shortcake*
Hawaiian Fruit Punch

*See index listing

....

Hilo Franks

Franks are seasoned with a tangy apricot sauce. Use sauce for glazing spitted duck or pork roast, too—

1 cup apricot preserves
½ 8-ounce can (½ cup) seasoned
   tomato sauce
⅓ cup vinegar
¼ cup cooking sherry
2 tablespoons soy sauce
2 tablespoons honey
1 tablespoon salad oil
1 teaspoon salt
1 teaspoon grated fresh gingerroot
   or ¼ teaspoon ground ginger

• • •

2 pounds frankfurters
1 No. 2 can pineapple
   slices, drained

For the sauce, combine first 9 ingredients. Score the frankfurters on the bias and broil slowly, turning and basting often with the sauce, till hot through and glazed.

Last few minutes grill pineapple rings: Place on grill; brush with basting sauce, broil and turn. Brush again with sauce. Heat remaining sauce to pass with franks. Go-with: a tossed salad. Serves 8 to 10.

Dunking Frankfurters

Sauce is sweet and hot — smacking-good on franks

2 cups finely chopped onions
¼ cup salad oil

• • •

1 14-ounce bottle (1¼ cups) catsup
½ cup water
¼ cup brown sugar
1 tablespoon vinegar
2 tablespoons Worcestershire sauce
½ teaspoon dry mustard
1 teaspoon salt
1 teaspoon liquid smoke

• • •

About 1½ dozen frankfurters

Cook onions in hot salad oil until almost tender. Add remaining ingredients except franks; simmer uncovered 15 minutes.

Meanwhile, score franks in corkscrew fashion, cutting round and round; roast on grill top or in wire broiler over hot coals. Drop into sauce to keep hot till serving time—or tuck them in toasted buns and spoon on sauce. Makes 9 servings.

Sloppy Joe Franks

Youngsters like this as is. Grownups dash in more hot pepper sauce—

½ cup chopped onion
2 tablespoons butter

• • •

1 pound (8 to 10) frankfurters,
   cut in thirds
1 can condensed tomato-rice soup
⅓ cup water
1 to 1½ tablespoons bottled steak
   sauce
1 teaspoon prepared mustard
4 drops bottled hot pepper sauce
Coney buns, toasted, buttered

Melt butter in skillet over coals. Add onion; cook till soft. Add remaining ingredients. Let bubble slowly without covering, about 15 minutes or till sauce is nice and thick. Stir once in a while near end of cooking. Ladle into buns. Makes 8 to 10.

Frank fix-ups for over the coals

Circle Pups (atop)—bias cut franks topped with hot kraut and mustard. Rafted Wieners (bottom)—franks filled with cheese and pickle; crossed with bacon strips.

Circle Pups

> 1 1-pound can (2 cups)
>   sauerkraut
> 1 tablespoon flour
> 1 teaspoon sage
>
> • • •
>
> 1 pound (8 to 10) frankfurters*
> 8 to 10 slices rye bread, buttered
> Prepared mustard

Drain kraut, reserving ½ cup juice. Mix flour, sage, and reserved juice; stir into the drained kraut. Heat and stir till mixture thickens. At ½-inch intervals, cut slits across franks, *going almost but not quite through.* Broil franks over hot coals until hot through—they'll curl as they cook. Place franks on bread; fill center with hot kraut; top with mustard.

*If using the chubby dinner-size franks, count on 2 to make each circle. Curve on bread making ends touch.

Rafted Wieners

Slit frankfurters lengthwise, *not quite through.* Grill over hot coals. Arrange bacon slices (2 per serving) on piece of foil, turning up edges to catch drippings; cook on grill top. Insert a strip of pickle and cheese in each frank and heat on foil a few minutes, place 2 or 3 franks crosswise on toasted and buttered coney buns. Lay 2 slices crisp bacon across the top.

Nutty Pups

A new favorite for all ages—

Broil franks to suit yourself. Serve in *hot* toasted buns spread with chunk-style peanut butter. Great when made with Frank Wrap-ups. Pass pickle relish.

Frank Wrap-ups

Slit frankfurters lengthwise to about ¼ inch from each end; stuff with pickle relish and wrap each with a bacon strip, anchoring ends with toothpicks. Broil over hot coals, turning once, till filling is hot and bacon crisped. (Remember to remove toothpicks anchoring bacon.)

Special burgers, tasty toppers

Aloha Burger (top) is glorified by a pineapple ring, and glazed with Island Sauce. Mountain Burger (bottom) is capped by an onion slice, a cascade of relish, and melty cheese.

Aloha Burgers

  1 9-ounce can pineapple slices
  1 pound ground beef
  1 teaspoon salt
  Dash pepper
  1 recipe Island Sauce

Drain pineapple, reserving 2 tablespoons syrup for sauce. Season meat with salt and pepper. Press a scant tablespoon of meat into center of each pineapple slice, overlapping meat on pineapple around center on both sides of slice so meat won't fall out while cooking. Shape remaining meat in 4 patties, slightly larger in diameter than the pineapple; broil burgers on grill over hot coals 12 to 15 minutes, turning once.

  Broil meat-filled pineapple slices, turning carefully and brushing with Island Sauce till meat is done and pineapple glazed. To assemble, place each burger atop a bun half or slice of toast. Top with pineapple burger. Peg with a kabob of cherry tomato and green olive.

  Island Sauce: Mix reserved pineapple syrup, ½ cup catsup, ¼ cup brown sugar, 2 teaspoons Worcestershire sauce, and a few drops liquid smoke; heat to boiling.

Mountain Burgers

  1 pound ground beef
  ¼ cup quick-cooking rolled oats
  2 tablespoons catsup
  2 tablespoons milk
  1 tablespoon prepared mustard
  1 slightly beaten egg
  1 teaspoon salt
  1 teaspoon monosodium glutamate
  ¼ teaspoon liquid smoke

  • • •

  4 thin onion slices
  ¼ cup drained pickle relish
  1 recipe 1-2-3 Cheese Sauce

Thoroughly combine meat, rolled oats, catsup, milk, mustard, egg, and seasonings; shape in 4 burgers. Grill over hot coals about 8 minutes; turn; top each with an onion slice and a mound of pickle relish; cook 7 minutes more or till done. Place on toasted buns; top with Cheese Sauce.

  1-2-3 Cheese Sauce: In saucepan, mix ⅓ cup process cheese spread, 2 tablespoons mayonnaise, and 1 tablespoon prepared mustard; heat at side of grill.

Favorite Grilled Hamburgers

1½ pounds ground beef*
2 tablespoons finely chopped onion
1 teaspoon salt
Dash pepper

. . .

1 cup catsup
2 teaspoons Worcestershire sauce
½ teaspoon celery salt
Dash bottled hot pepper sauce
6 hamburger buns, split, toasted,
   and buttered

Mix meat, onion, salt, and pepper. Lightly pat into 6 burgers, about ½ inch thick. Broil over hot coals about 6 minutes, turn and broil 4 minutes longer or till done to your liking. Meanwhile combine next 4 ingredients for sauce and heat on grill. When burgers are done, brush both sides with the sauce and serve in hot buns. Pass extra sauce and prepared mustard.

*If meat is lean have 4 ounces suet ground with this amount. Juicier!

Giant Burgers

3 tablespoons instant minced onion
1 6-ounce can evaporated milk
1½ pounds ground beef
1½ teaspoons salt
Dash pepper
1 to 2 tablespoons steak sauce

Soak instant onion in evaporated milk a few minutes. Thoroughly combine meat, seasonings, and milk-onion mixture. Shape in five 4-inch patties, about ¾ inch thick. Brush both sides with salad oil or melted margarine. Broil over slow coals 5 minutes; turn, cook 3 to 4 minutes longer or till done. Serve with hot toasted hamburger buns. Makes 5 servings.

Pennyburgers

3 or 4 frankfurters, sliced thin
1 pound ground beef
1 teaspoon salt
Dash pepper
⅛ cup evaporated milk

Mix ingredients; shape 6 patties, about ½-inch thick; spread both sides with butter.

Broil over hot coals, turning once, about 13 to 15 minutes total cooking time. Serve in toasted buns. Pass catsup, mustard, and hamburger relish. Makes 6 servings.

Burgundy Beefburgers

2 pounds ground chuck
1 cup soft bread crumbs
1 egg
¼ cup red cooking wine (not sweet)
2 tablespoons sliced green onions
1 teaspoon salt
Dash pepper

In large bowl, toss all ingredients with a fork until well mixed. Shape in 8 patties, about ½-inch thick. Broil over hot coals, turning once and brushing frequently with Burgundy Sauce, 13 to 15 minutes total cooking time or till of desired doneness. Heat remaining sauce to pass. Serves 8.

Burgundy Sauce: Cook 2 tablespoons sliced scallions in ½ cup butter till just tender. Add ¼ cup red cooking wine.

Hot Dogie-burgers

1 slightly beaten egg
1 pound ground beef*
1 tablespoon Worcestershire sauce
¾ teaspoon salt
¾ teaspoon seasoned salt
6 frankfurters (the long thins)
6 coney buns, split, toasted, buttered

Combine first 5 ingredients, mixing well. Completely encase each frank with beef mixture; spread outside with soft butter. Grill over hot coals about 13 minutes, turning often to cook all sides. Serve in hot buns with hot-dog relish, prepared mustard, and catsup. Makes 6 servings.

*If beef is lean, have 2 or 3 ounces suet ground with each pound.

Broil on foil. No grill losses—

No broiler basket? Grids too far apart for small meats? Tear off a strip of foil the size of your grill top. With two-tined fork, puncture foil at 2-inch intervals. Careful—don't tear. Turn up a half-inch edge on your "pan" all around. Lay meat on hot foil. (Holes let heat up  and fat drippings out so meat broils instead of sizzling.) Other pluses: You can throw your foil "pan" away—and grill's easy to clean!

Dad's ready with the Whopper-burgers. Break out the buns!

Whopper-burgers

Two juicy meat patties in one—and there's a surprise in between—

2 pounds ground beef
Salt and pepper
Prepared mustard

• • •

Pickle Filling: pickle relish and
½-inch cubes of sharp process
American cheese*

Shape patties as directed below. Set half the patties aside for "lids." Sprinkle remaining patties with salt and pepper, then spread with prepared mustard, leaving ½-inch margin for sealing. Top with a mound of Pickle Filling. Cover the filling with "lids," sealing edges well.

Place on greased grill or spread both sides with soft butter or margarine. Season top side with salt and pepper.

Broil over hot coals about 10 minutes; turn; broil about 10 minutes more or till done to your liking. Season second side. Slip patties into hot buttered buns. Makes 5 Whopper-burgers.

*Or, fill each with a thin onion slice, and a round of smoky cheese.

*See index listing

All-American Barbecue

Whopper-burgers
Beanpot*   Calico Potato Salad*
Pickles
Fudge Sundaes
Ice-cold Pop   Hot Coffee

*See index listing

Two-faced Hamburgers

2 pounds ground beef
½ cup extra-hot catsup
2 teaspoons salt
1 loaf French bread
Prepared mustard and mayonnaise

Mix meat, catsup, and salt. Cut the bread in ¾- to 1-inch slices. Spread both sides of each slice with prepared mustard, then with mayonnaise, and last with generous amount of meat mixture (on each "face" of bread). Broil in wire broiler over hot coals; turn once. Makes 8 to 10.

Here's the straight dope on making super-duper Whopper-burgers.

Using a ⅓-cup measure, divide ground beef in 10 mounds. Flatten each mound between squares of waxed paper to a 4-inch patty.

For a leakproof seal and a good "figure," press together edges of burgers all around on top side, then turn and seal edges again.

Big flavor, small cost— Sure to be a hit at your barbecue is Chef's Chuck Roast. Grilled meat bubbles to perfection in Quick Bordelaise Sauce. Pass French-fried onions, green salad, pie, coffee.

Bargains to barbecue

Chef's Chuck Roast

Choose a 4- to 5-pound chuck pot roast, about 2 inches thick. Trim off excess fat. Let meat come to room temperature. Slash the fat edge. Use instant meat tenderizer according to label directions.

Brown meat on grill, about 2 inches from hot coals, a total of 30 minutes, turning frequently.* Place meat in Dutch oven or large skillet and pour Quick Bordelaise Sauce over; cover; cook *slowly* about 1 hour. Makes 8 to 10 servings.

*For *rare*, serve *now* and pass sauce.

Quick Bordelaise Sauce

2 carrots, chopped fine
3 tablespoons instant minced onion
1 3-ounce can (⅜ cup) broiled sliced
   mushrooms, drained
⅓ to ½ cup cooking claret
1 can beef gravy
1 tablespoon lemon juice
½ teaspoon monosodium glutamate

Cook carrots tender in ¼ cup butter. Add onion, mushrooms, claret. Simmer uncovered about 5 minutes. Add remaining ingredients; simmer 5 minutes more.

Big Beef Sandwich

3 pounds chuck or round steak,
    about 2 inches thick
Instant meat tenderizer
½ cup soft butter or margarine
2 tablespoons prepared mustard
1 tablespoon prepared horseradish
1 loaf French bread, about 18
    inches long
Freshly ground coarse pepper

Slash fat edges of steak. Use meat tenderizer, according to label directions. Broil on grill, about 2 inches from coals, a total of 25 to 30 minutes, turning frequently—do not overcook.

Blend butter, mustard, and horseradish. Cut bread lengthwise in half; toast both sides on grill and keep *hot* in foil while you carve the steak: Slice meat with sharp knife *diagonally across the grain*, at about a 30° angle, making *very thin* slices. Spread cut sides of bread (both halves) *generously* with the mustard butter. Overlap meat slices across bottom half of loaf, making double or triple layers. Dash with coarse pepper. Drizzle meat juices from carving platter over the steak slices. Add top half of loaf; cut on the bias into 8 sandwiches.

Camp Stew

2 pounds boneless lean beef chuck or
    stew meat, cut in 1½-inch cubes
3 cups water
½ cup cooking sherry
1 6-ounce can tomato paste
1 tablespoon salt
¼ teaspoon pepper
1 teaspoon Worcestershire sauce
2 bay leaves
2 onions, quartered
    •   •   •
6 carrots, cut in eighths
4 potatoes, pared and quartered
1 1-pound can (2 cups) green Limas,
    drained
1 8-ounce can (1 cup) whole
    kernel corn, drained

Brown meat in small amount hot fat. Add water and next 7 ingredients; cover and simmer about 1¼ hours. Add carrots and potatoes; cook 30 minutes longer or till tender. Add Limas and corn; heat till hot through. Makes 6 to 8 servings.

Patio Fiesta Dinner

½ cup finely chopped onion
1 clove garlic, minced
3 tablespoons olive oil
1 tablespoon flour
1 10-ounce can tomato puree
½ cup water
1 to 2 tablespoons chili powder
1 teaspoon salt
¼ teaspoon oregano
¼ teaspoon cumin
    •   •   •
1 pound boneless lean beef chuck or
    beef stew meat, cut in 1-inch cubes
1 12-ounce can (1½ cups) whole
    kernel corn, drained
1 10-ounce package frozen baby Limas
1 onion, sliced, separated in rings
1 green pepper, sliced in rings
1 cup shredded sharp process cheese
¼ cup finely chopped onion
1 6-ounce package corn chips

Cook ½ cup chopped onion and the garlic in 3 tablespoons olive oil till tender; stir in flour. Add tomato, water, and seasonings; simmer 10 minutes, stirring occasionally.

Tear off four 12-inch lengths of 18-inch-wide foil. On each, place one-fourth of the meat, top with vegetables. Drizzle each serving with about ½ cup sauce. Bring edges of foil up, and leaving room for expansion of steam, seal well with double fold. Place packets on grill and cook over the coals till meat is tender, about 1½ hours, turning once.

When serving, cut a big crisscross in top of packets and fold foil back. Sprinkle each dinner with cheese, chopped onion, and corn chips. Makes 4 servings.

Stew-pendous!

Chilled Cantaloupe Wedges
Camp Stew
Grilled Garlic-bread Slices*
Lettuce Wedges with
Blue-Cheese Dressing
Powwow Sundaes*
Cold Milk   Hot Coffee

*See index listing

Kettle Barbecued Pot Roast

Select a 6- to 9-pound beef pot roast, 3 to 4 inches thick. Rub it with olive oil, salt, and pepper. Place on grill top over coals and sear meat on both sides.

Baste with a sauce of sour cream spiked with garlic powder and prepared horseradish to suit your taste. Cover barbecue kettle with lid (or lower smoker hood). Cook slowly about 15 minutes per pound for medium rare. Every 15 minutes of roasting time, turn meat and baste with sour-cream sauce.

Cracked-pepper Steak

Select a 4-pound chuck steak, 2½ to 3 inches thick. Slash fat edges. Use instant meat tenderizer on steak according to label directions. Press cracked or coarsely ground pepper into both sides of meat (takes about 3 tablespoons).

Broil on grill about 3 inches from coals, 35 to 50 minutes, turning frequently with tongs. To serve, slice *diagonally across the grain*, at about a 30° angle—keep the slices thin. Makes 6 to 8 servings.

Steak Sandwiches with Johnny Appleseed Sauce

Sauce is seasoned catsup mellowed by applesauce—

1 medium onion, sliced thin
¼ cup salad oil
1 cup canned applesauce
1 cup catsup
1 tablespoon sugar
2 tablespoons Worcestershire sauce
1 tablespoon lemon juice
½ teaspoon salt
½ teaspoon crushed oregano
6 cube steaks
6 hamburger buns, split, toasted, and buttered

In large skillet, cook onion in hot oil till tender but not brown; add applesauce, catsup, and seasonings. Heat, stirring occasionally, till bubbling. Remove from heat; add steaks, turning to coat, and let stand 15 minutes. Lift out steaks and broil quickly over hot coals, about 1 or 2 minutes per side, brushing with barbecue sauce after turning. Slip steaks into hot buns, ladling extra sauce on meat. Serves 6.

Saucy Lamb Riblets

Before you cook the ribs in this gently seasoned sauce, give them a touch of smoke—

3 to 4 pounds lamb riblets, cut in serving pieces
Salt and pepper

• • •

¾ cup catsup
¾ cup water
½ cup chopped onion
2 tablespoons brown sugar
3 tablespoons lemon juice
3 tablespoons Worcestershire sauce
2 tablespoons vinegar
1½ teaspoons monosodium glutamate
¾ teaspoon salt
Dash bottled hot pepper sauce

Brown riblets* on grill over hot coals with hickory added, turning often (takes about 15 to 20 minutes). Season with salt and pepper. Meanwhile, combine remaining ingredients. Transfer meat to skillet and pour the sauce over. Cover tightly; simmer (don't boil) 1 hour or till tender. Remove excess fat. Pass bowl of sauce with riblets. Offer lemon wedges. Makes 4 or 5 servings.

*Before browning meat, place a foil "boat" (double thickness) over the coals to catch drippings. Remove after browning.

El Paso Beans

1 pound (about 2⅔ cups) dry pinto beans
1 pound lean beef stew meat, cut in ½-inch cubes
1 teaspoon salt
½ teaspoon monosodium glutamate
½ teaspoon crushed oregano
4 ounces salt pork, diced
1 cup chopped onion
2 8-ounce cans (2 cups) seasoned tomato sauce
3 cloves garlic, minced
1 to 3 teaspoons finely minced hot pickled peppers

Rinse beans, drain. Add 6 cups cold water; cover and bring to boiling. Reduce heat and simmer 1½ hours. Add meat and remaining ingredients. Cover and simmer about 1½ hours, stirring occasionally—beans should have burst, giving soup a nice consistency. Salt to taste. Serve in soup bowls. Makes 8 servings.

Barbecued Bologna (*See cover*)

1 3- to 4-pound big Bologna, unsliced
1 cup catsup
⅛ cup butter or margarine, melted
1½ tablespoons Worcestershire sauce
1½ tablespoons golden brown
    prepared mustard
1½ teaspoons onion salt

Score Bologna with diagonal lines about ¼ inch deep. Anchor on spit, attach to grill. (Place foil drip pan below, if your barbecue does not have a built-in drip catcher.) Cook on rotisserie with hood down over medium coals for 1¼ hours or till heated through and browned.

Meanwhile, combine remaining ingredients for sauce; brush on Bologna frequently the last 15 minutes of cooking.

Slice meat about ¼ inch thick; serve between toasted hamburger buns, with remaining sauce heated and spooned over.

Cheese-frosted Luncheon Meat

Anchor canned luncheon meat on spit. Blend 2 parts triple-use cheese spread and 1 part Dijon-style prepared mustard; slather on all sides of meat.

Grill over hot coals till golden brown. Slice and serve with dill pickle slices on toasted rolls. Pass extra sauce.

Spicy Pork Sandwiches

1 12-ounce bottle (1¼ cups) extra-
    hot catsup
½ cup finely chopped onion
⅛ cup finely chopped green pepper
1 tablespoon brown sugar
1 tablespoon mixed pickling spice
1 teaspoon salt
1½ teaspoons dry mustard
Dash bottled hot pepper sauce

• • •

3 to 4 cups shredded cooked fresh pork
    (2 to 2½ pounds before roasting)
10 to 12 hamburger buns, toasted
    and buttered

Combine first 8 ingredients, tying pickling spice in cheesecloth bag. Cover and simmer 15 minutes. Remove spice bag and add shredded meat to sauce. Cover; simmer 10 minutes or till heated through. Serve in hot buns. Makes 10 to 12 sandwiches.

Skillet Beans 'n Franks

In skillet, melt 2 tablespoons butter; add 1 cup diced tomato, ½ teaspoon crushed oregano and ¼ teaspoon garlic powder; cook a minute to blend flavors. Add two 1-pound cans beans and franks in tomato sauce. Heat over slow coals, stirring often, till hot. Trim with parsley. Makes 6 servings.

Island Teriyaki cooks to tasty perfection on hibachi. Terrific!

Combine ½ cup soy sauce, ¼ cup brown sugar, 2 tablespoons olive oil, 1 teaspoon dry ginger, ½ teaspoon monosodium glutamate, ¼ teaspoon cracked pepper, and 2 cloves garlic, minced; mix well.

Cut 1½ pounds top sirloin steak in strips ¼ inch thick by 1 inch wide. Add to sauce; stir to coat. Let stand 2 hours.

Lace meat in accordion style on skewers. Add a water chestnut at end of each. Broil over hot coals 10 to 12 minutes, turning frequently, basting with marinade. Serves 4 or 5.

Birds, blue-ribbon ways

Chicken Broilercue

The jelly glaze is superb—glossy, flavorful

¼ cup salad oil
¼ cup cooking sauterne
¼ cup chicken broth
2 tablespoons lemon juice
2 tablespoons apple jelly
1 teaspoon salt
½ teaspoon monosodium glutamate
1 teaspoon snipped parsley
½ teaspoon prepared mustard
½ teaspoon Worcestershire sauce
Dash *each* celery seed, rosemary,
  and pepper
• • •
2 ready-to-cook broilers (2 to 2½
  pounds each), halved lengthwise

Combine all ingredients except chicken; beat out lumps of jelly with rotary beater. Brush chicken with the sauce and place bone side down on grill. Broil over slow coals, turning occasionally and basting frequently, about 1 hour or till meat is tender and skin is crisp and dark. Serves 4.

Flying Drumsticks

No fussing over who rates the drumsticks—everyone gets two—

¼ cup catsup
2 to 3 tablespoons lemon juice
2 tablespoons soy sauce
¼ cup salad oil
½ teaspoon monosodium glutamate
• • •
12 chicken drumsticks

Combine first 5 ingredients for marinade, mixing well. Add chicken legs and stir to coat. Refrigerate overnight or let stand at room temperature 2 hours, spooning sauce over occasionally.

Place drumsticks in wire broil basket. Grill over slow coals about 25 minutes, basting with marinade now and then. Turn and grill other side about 20 minutes or till tender, basting with marinade. Serves 6.

Gourmet Marinated Chicken

1 envelope herb salad-dressing mix
1 envelope garlic salad-dressing mix
½ cup cooking sherry
⅔ cup salad oil
2 ready-to-cook 2-pound broiler
  chickens, split in half lengthwise

Combine first 4 ingredients for marinade, mixing well; brush chicken to coat. Place chicken in shallow baking dish and drizzle with remaining marinade. Refrigerate overnight or let stand at room temperature 2 hours, spooning marinade over often.

Place chicken on grill with bone side or inside nearest the coals. Broil over slow coals, brushing chicken frequently with marinade. When bone side is well browned, 20 to 30 minutes, turn skin side down and cook about 20 to 30 minutes longer or till done, brushing with marinade. *Doneness test:* Shake hands with the drumstick—leg should move easily. Thickest parts of chicken should feel very soft. Serves 4.

Whirlibird Chickens

Select ready-to-cook fryers, about 2½ pounds each. Skewer neck skin to back; loop cord over skewer and tie wings *firmly* to body. Dovetail birds on spit (use 2 holding forks per bird). Tie legs, tail to rod. Test balance. Brush birds with Chicken Basting Sauce. Season; dash with paprika.

Attach spit, turn on motor. Have medium coals at back of firebox and a drip pan directly under the chicken. Chicken is self-basting, but for spunk, or if birds look dry, brush with basting sauce or salad oil last half hour. Allow about 1½ hours with hood down, a little longer with no hood.

Check doneness near end of cooking: When done, drumsticks move easily; thick part of drumstick feels very soft.

Chicken Basting Sauce: Combine one 5-ounce bottle (⅔ cup) Worcestershire sauce, ½ cup salad oil, ¼ to ⅓ cup lemon juice, and 1 clove garlic, minced.

Rotisserie Turkey

Allow ½ pound of ready-to-cook turkey per person. Rub inside of bird with 1 tablespoon salt. Truss turkey and balance on spit—drumstick holding fork is a dandy helper. (Or use a rotary roast rack and omit trussing.) Brush bird with salad oil. Adjust on rotisserie—have slow coals at back of barbecue, and a foil drip pan under revolving bird.

Roast large turkey about 15 minutes per pound with hood down, longer with no hood. A small turkey may take up to 25 or 30 minutes per pound.* For smoke flavor, toss damp hickory on coals. (If you like, brush bird with your favorite barbecue sauce during last half hour of cooking.)

About 20 minutes before roasting time is up, snip cord that holds drumsticks to spit. Test doneness as for Whirlibird Chickens. Before carving, let turkey rest 15 minutes.

*Times are approximate only. Allow plenty of time your first try and experiment.

Hickory Smoked Turkey

Dusky-toned and delicious hot or cold—

1 10-pound ready-to-cook turkey
¼ cup salad oil
½ cup salt
1 cup vinegar
¼ cup pepper
2 teaspoons finely chopped parsley

Rinse bird; pat dry with paper towels. Make a paste of oil and salt; rub ¼ *cup* of mixture inside of bird. Truss turkey and balance on spit or use rotary roast rack. Brush with salad oil.

Have slow coals at back of barbecue, a drip pan under revolving bird. For moisture, place a pan of water at end of firebox.

Roast, hood down, for one hour. Then brush with sauce made by combining the remaining salt with vinegar, pepper, parsley. Toss damp hickory chips on coals.

Roast, hood down, 3½ to 4 hours longer. Baste bird every 30 minutes or so (also check on fire, hickory, and water in pan).

About 20 minutes before roasting time is up, snip cord that holds drumsticks. Test doneness as for Whirlibird Chickens. Let rest 15 minutes before carving.

Luscious Cornish Hens

4 1-pound Rock Cornish hens, thawed
1 cup finely chopped California walnuts, or roasted or boiled Italian chestnuts
¼ cup olive oil
1 teaspoon salt
1 teaspoon celery salt
1 teaspoon poultry seasoning
½ teaspoon rosemary
½ cup butter or margarine, melted
Salt and freshly ground pepper

Rinse birds; pat dry with paper towels. Combine next 6 ingredients; rub *half* of mixture inside birds. Truss birds; mount on spit, securing with holding forks. Rub birds with remaining nut mixture; let stand 15 minutes. Roast over coals 1 to 1¼ hours or till tender—after 15 minutes, brush now and then with butter. Sprinkle with salt and grind pepper over; continue cooking 10 minutes. Makes 4 servings.

Cornish Capons, Tangerine

Get acquainted with Rock Cornish capons (brothers of the dainty hens). They weigh 6 or 7 pounds each. Truss and spit roast as you would chickens or small turkeys.

During last 5 to 10 minutes of roasting time, brush with *Tangerine-Currant Glaze:* In small saucepan, break up 1 cup currant jelly. Stir in one 6-ounce can frozen tangerine concentrate, 1 teaspoon dry mustard, dash ginger and dash hot pepper sauce. Heat and stir till mixture is smooth.

One to remember

Olives-in-Bacon Appetizers*
Luscious Cornish Hens
Calico Potato Salad*
Bibb Lettuce with
Vinegar-Oil Dressing
Grill-warmed Rolls   Butter
Make-your-own Sundaes
Hot Coffee

*See index listing

Fishermen's favorites

Fish in Corn Husks

Pan fish skip the pan, roast right in coals—

In the cavity of each cleaned fish place a lump of butter (cut chunks 1-inch wide from a ¼-pound stick) and give fish a generous squirt of lemon juice. Sprinkle with salt and fresh-ground pepper.

Wrap each in a whole de-silked corn husk;* tie with string at silk end. Place on bed of hot coals; top with more coals. Cook about 15 minutes or till fish flakes when tested with fork. Pass extra butter.

*If husks are quite dry, first soak in water about 5 minutes.

Fish and Bacon variation: Sprinkle fish cavity with salt and fresh-ground pepper. Place a bacon strip down each side of fish, wrap in corn husks. Continue as above.

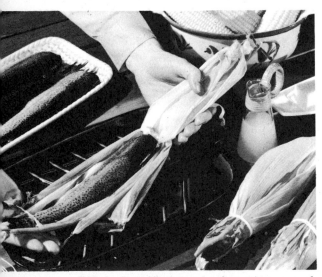

Fish in Corn Husks make the eating as much fun as the catching (or buy ½-pound fish). Buttery sauce melts inside as fish cooks.

Bacon-stuffed Trout

2 eggs
1 tablespoon cream or milk
1 teaspoon dried parsley flakes
1 clove garlic, minced
½ teaspoon allspice
• • •
8 cleaned brook trout
8 or 16 strips grilled bacon

Beat together first 5 ingredients to blend. Coat fish inside and out with mixture. Put 1 or 2 strips bacon in each trout and place in greased wire broil basket or on greased hot grill. Cook over hot coals 20 minutes or till fish flakes with fork—turn once. Serve with lemon wedges. Makes 8 servings.

Herbed Fish Grill

1 1½- to 2-pound fish (whitefish,
    trout or similar fresh-water fish)
½ cup butter
1 teaspoon salt and dash pepper
1 teaspoon coriander seed, crushed
¼ teaspoon cardamom
2 tablespoons lemon juice
1 cup yogurt
Fresh fennel, dill, or other leafy herb

Salt cleaned fish. Melt butter; mix in seasonings, lemon juice, and yogurt. Coat fish inside and out with mixture. Place in wire broil basket and cook over coals till fish browns on both sides and flakes when tested with a fork (about 25 to 30 minutes)—brush often with the sauce.

Ten minutes before end of cooking time, make bed of leafy herbs on grill top; lay fish atop. Grill till herbs smolder and flavor the fish, turning once. Heat remaining sauce to pass. Serves 4 to 6.

Fillets with Caper Sauce

Select inch-thick fish fillets, fresh or frozen. Thaw, if frozen. Brush with salad oil or melted butter. Place in greased wire broil basket or on grill. Cook over hot coals till fish flakes with a fork—turn once. Serve with Caper Sauce.

Caper Sauce: Mix 1 cup mayonnaise, ¼ cup drained chopped sour pickles, and 1½ teaspoons *each* prepared mustard and chopped parsley. Makes 1½ cups sauce.

Company meats

Rotisserie Roast
(*Beef, Pork, or Lamb*)

Choose a roast weighing at least 3½ to 4 pounds so it will still be juicy when cooked. Have meatman tie roast at 1-inch intervals with heavy cord to make compact. (If meat is lean, have outside covered with a layer of fat and trussed securely.)

Let meat come to room temperature before starting to cook. Balance on spit. Insert meat thermometer into heaviest part of roast, so tip is in center of meat, but not touching bone, fat, or spit.

Arrange hot coals at back of firebox. Coals should be a little less hot than for broiling. (Use *slow* coals if you're cooking with hood closed.) Knock off the gray ash. Attach spit, turn on motor. (Have drip pan under roast unless barbecue unit has built-in drip catcher. (Make drip pan of a double thickness of heavy-duty foil. It should be as long as your grill, half as wide, with 1½-inch sides, mitered corners.)

Cook roast till done — see chart below. (Allow a little extra time for boned rolled roasts.) Roasts are self-basting.

When roast is done, let it firm up 15 to 20 minutes before carving. You may lower firebox to stop cooking and let roast continue to rotate, or transfer to platter.

Rotisserie roasting guide

Kind of roast	Approximate cooking time*	Reading of thermometer
Beef		
Rare	2 to 2½ hrs.	140°
Medium	2½ to 3 hrs.	160°
Well-done	3 to 4 hrs.	170°
Pork, fresh	2 to 3½ hrs.	185°
Lamb		
Medium	1½ to 2 hrs.	175°
Well-done	2 to 2½ hrs.	180°

For 4- to 6-pound standing roast at room temperature.

Peanut-buttered Pork Roast

When Rotisserie Roast pork is well-done (meat thermometer reads 185°), brush roast with mixture of ¼ cup peanut butter and ¼ cup orange juice and continue cooking and basting about 15 to 20 minutes.

Roast Beef with Herb Butter

Serve Rotisserie Roast beef with a dab of Herb Butter on each slice (it's potent!).

Herb Butter: Blend ½ cup soft butter with 2 teaspoons seasoned salt, 1 teaspoon *fines herbes*, ¼ teaspoon cracked pepper, and a few drops bottled hot pepper sauce.

Orange-stuffed Leg of Lamb

It's flavor-stuffed — with fruit, herbs, garlic —

1 lemon
2 oranges
. . .
1 6- or 7-pound leg of lamb, boned
2 cloves garlic, crushed
Salt and coarsely ground pepper
. . .
1 cup water
¼ cup (½ stick) butter or margarine
1 teaspoon whole thyme
1 8-ounce package (3½ cups)
   herb-seasoned stuffing

Cut peel in *paper-thin* strips from lemon and *1* orange. (Easy with vegetable parer.) Section both oranges.

Rub inside surface of meat with crushed garlic and sprinkle with salt and pepper; scatter peels over.

Bring water, butter, and thyme to boiling; when butter has melted, drizzle over stuffing, tossing to mix. Spoon about 2 cups stuffing* on half the meat (the short way) and press double row of orange sections down center; fold other half of meat over stuffing to make a square roast. Skewer the three open sides; lace shut. Tie tightly with string at 1½-inch intervals.

Center roast on spit and continue as for Rotisserie Roast (allow 2 to 2½ hours cooking time). Makes 10 to 12 servings.

*About 45 minutes before roast is done, wrap remainder of stuffing in foil; heat on grill, turning package occasionally.

Spinning Ham

Round, boneless, fully cooked ham

• • •

1 cup extra-hot catsup
⅔ cup orange marmalade
¼ cup finely chopped onion
¼ cup salad oil
2 tablespoons lemon juice
2 to 3 teaspoons mustard

Remove casing from ham, if it has one. Score. Tie with cord if necessary. Center lengthwise on spit and roast as for Rotisserie Roast, page 21, about 20 minutes per pound, or to temperature of 130°. Combine remaining ingredients; brush on ham last ½ hour. Pass extra glaze with ham.

Chili Grill-roasted Lamb

Have a 6-pound leg of lamb boned and flattened. Marinate 2 hours at room temperature in a mixture of: 1 cup salad oil, ¼ cup wine vinegar, 1 tablespoon salt, ¼ teaspoon *each* salt and garlic powder.

Mix 2 cups chopped onion, 2½ cups chili sauce, ½ cup lemon juice, ⅓ cup salad oil, 2 tablespoons vinegar, 2 teaspoons hot pepper sauce, 1 teaspoon minced canned green chiles, 1 tablespoon brown sugar, 1 teaspoon *each* salt and dry mustard, 1 bay leaf crushed. Simmer 20 minutes.

Roast meat on *grill* about 2 hours; turn every 15 minutes and baste with chili-sauce mixture. Slice cross-grain. Serves 8 to 10.

Swank Porterhouse Steak

It's the ultimate in outdoor chefing—tender pink steak with a crunchy band of onion in the center, mushroom-butter sauce atop! Pass foiled potatoes, crisp green salad.

Grilled Steaks

Choose tender steaks, about 1 inch thick. (Rib steaks are easier than T-bones on your budget.) Remove meat from refrigerator an hour or so before broiling so it is at room temperature. Slash fat edge at intervals to keep steaks flat.

When coals are *hot*, tap off gray ash with fire tongs. Let grill top heat, then grease it and put on the steaks (orders for "rare" go on last). When you see little bubbles on top side of steaks, they are ready to turn (heat forces the juices to the uncooked surface). Flip steaks with tongs and pancake turner—piercing with a fork wastes good meat juices. Season steak right after turning *or* as it comes off the grill. Broil second side less long than first—turn only once. For 1-inch steaks cooked medium-rare, allow about 13 to 15 minutes *total* broiling time.

For char flavor: Sear Steak on one side by lowering grill top close to coals for 2 or 3 minutes, then raise grill to finish same side. Turn steak, and sear second side; again raise grill and complete the cooking.

Swank Porterhouse Steak

1 2½- to 3-pound Porterhouse or
   sirloin steak, about 2 inches thick
     •   •   •
¾ cup finely chopped Bermuda onion
2 cloves garlic, minced
Dash *each* salt, pepper, celery salt
3 tablespoons cooking claret
2 tablespoons soy sauce
     •   •   •
¼ cup butter or margarine
1 3-ounce can (⅔ cup) broiled
   sliced mushrooms, drained

Slash fat edge of steak—don't cut into meat. Slitting from fat side, cut pocket in each side of lean, *almost* to bone.

Combine onion and garlic, salt, pepper, and celery salt; fill pockets in steak. Mix claret and soy sauce; brush on steak.

Grill over hot coals a total of 25 minutes or till done to your liking, turning once—brush occasionally with soy mixture.

Heat butter and mushrooms, pour over steak. Slice across grain and serve sizzling! Makes 4 delicious servings.

Ham Barbecue

Western Starter*
Barbecue-glazed Ham
Foiled Yams (see Foiled Spuds*)
Spring Coleslaw*
Grill-warmed Corn Sticks   Butter
Hot Banana Shortcake*   Coffee

*See index listing

Barbecue-glazed Ham

¾ cup catsup
3 tablespoons brown sugar
1½ tablespoons Dijon-style mustard
2 tablespoons Worcestershire sauce
2 tablespoons lemon juice
2 teaspoons chili powder
     •   •   •
2 ½-inch slices fully cooked ham
   (about 1½ pounds)

Mix first 6 ingredients for sauce. Slash fat edge of ham. Brush meat liberally with sauce; let stand 1 hour. Grill over coals 5 to 6 minutes per side, turning once and brushing with sauce. Serves 4 to 6.

Orange-glazed Ham 'n Pineapple

Cooking sherry and fines herbes give heavenly aroma, dandy flavor —

¼ cup frozen orange-juice concentrate
¼ cup cooking sherry
1 teaspoon dry mustard
¼ teaspoon *fines herbes*
     •   •   •
1 1-inch slice fully cooked ham
   (about 1½ pounds)
4 to 6 canned pineapple slices

Combine first 4 ingredients for sauce; brush on ham. Grill over hot coals 6 to 8 minutes on each side or till browned, basting frequently. Last few minutes, grill pineapple slices 2 to 3 minutes on each side or till browned, basting frequently with sauce. Makes 4 to 6 servings.

Spit-barbecued Ribs

Lace meaty loin back ribs or spareribs in accordion style on spit, using holding forks—check tips below for how-to.

Arrange hot coals at back of firebox and a drip pan in front of coals and under ribs (unless barbecue has a built-in drip catcher). See directions for making drip pan in recipe for Rotisserie Roast, page 21. Let ribs rotate over *slow* coals 1 hour or till meat is well-done (no pink when snipped between bones).

Last 20 minutes, baste well with Real-hot Sauce or Ginger Glaze, and, if you like, add hickory to coals for smoke flavor (see tips). Allow 3 pounds ribs for 4 people.

Real-hot Sauce

> 1 cup extra-hot catsup
> ½ cup water
> ¼ cup molasses
> ¼ cup vinegar
> 3 tablespoons Worcestershire sauce
> 2 teaspoons salt
> ½ teaspoon dry mustard
> ¼ teaspoon fresh-ground pepper
> 2 cloves garlic, minced

Mix ingredients well and let stand to mellow at least a few hours.

Stir before using. Makes enough sauce to baste 4 pounds ribs.

Rib tips: Skewering, hickory use

To thread spareribs on spit: Have meatman saw ribs in two strips, each about 3 inches wide. Beginning with narrow end of ribs,  run spit through middle, lacing accordion style. For balance on spit, start the second strip at wide end, third at narrow end, and so on. Have a holding fork for each slab of ribs.

For hickory flavor: Soak hickory hunks, crosscuts, or bark in water 1 hour. Or, dampen sawdust, flakes, or chips when you start the fire. (Mahogany chips and fruitwood are also good for smoke.) Add to coals last 20 to 30 minutes.

To "hickory-smoke" on open grill: Wrap fistful of dry hickory chips in foil. Puncture top of package with fork; place on hot coals. Soon smoke will puff out, continuing ½ hour.

Ginger Glaze

Combine 2 tablespoons cornstarch, ⅔ cup brown sugar, ⅔ cup soy sauce, 6 tablespoons *finely* chopped candied ginger, 2 cloves garlic, crushed, and ¼ cup vinegar. For best flavor, let stand overnight. Makes enough glaze to baste 4 pounds ribs.

On-the-grill Spareribs

> 2 envelopes herb- or French-salad-
>   dressing mix
> ½ cup dark corn syrup
> ¼ cup vinegar
> 3 tablespoons brown sugar
> 4 pounds lean spareribs

For basting sauce, combine salad-dressing mix, corn syrup, vinegar, and brown sugar; stir well and set aside.

Place ribs bone side down on grill over *slow* coals. (Watch the fire—ribs tend to dry out and char.) Broil about 20 minutes; turn meaty side down and leave briefly until nicely browned. Turn meat side up again and broil about 20 minutes longer.

Now brush meat side with basting sauce (and add hickory, if desired—see tips, left). Continue to broil without turning, 20 to 30 minutes or till done (no pink), basting occasionally with the sauce. At the last, brush sauce on both sides of ribs, and let broil 2 or 3 minutes on each side. Serves 4.

Roast Pork Chops

> Rib or loin pork chops, cut
>   1 to 1¼ inches thick
> 1 cup chopped onion
> 1 clove garlic, minced
> 1 cup water
> ¾ cup catsup
> ⅓ cup lemon juice
> 3 tablespoons sugar
> 2 tablespoons Worcestershire sauce
> 1 tablespoon prepared mustard
> 2 teaspoons salt
> ¼ teaspoon hot pepper sauce

Lock chops in spit basket. Turn over *slow* coals 45 minutes to 1 hour, or till well-done. Last 20 minutes, baste with Sauce, and add hickory to coals (see tips).

Sauce: Cook onion and garlic in ¼ cup salad oil till just tender. Add remaining ingredients; simmer uncovered 15 minutes.

Over-the-coals kabobs

Kabobing for swordsmen

Call it "kebab" or "shashlik," "en brochette," or "teriyaki"—it's dinner cooked on a stick—always a favorite.

Kabob choices: Select quick-cooking meats and vegetables. When different kinds of food share the same skewer, choose those that cook same time.

How-to: Leave space between tidbits on skewer, so heat reaches all. Exception: For *rare* beef, push close.

Slosh vegetables with melted butter or salad oil, before and during cooking. Or baste with meat marinade.

Lucky the chef who boasts motorized skewers! For hand turning, use kabob frame, or support on bricks.

Cook kabobs over *hot* coals so food stays moist, yet browns to a turn.

Serving from a sword: To "unhand" a skewerful, put a 2-tined fork above the 2 or 3 chunks of food nearest tip and push off. Repeat. (If you try to push off more, you'll squash vegetables.)

What to eat with kabobs: Shish kebab calls for fluffy buttered rice, or buckwheat groats, or pilaf. Partner beef kabobs with baked potatoes, and ham or luncheon meat with yams or hominy.

Make-your-own Kabobs

Set out bowls of ingredients (see below) and let each guest thread his own skewer. Broil over *hot* coals to medium rare, basting often with marinade.

Meats: Marinated Lamb Squares and Marinated Beef Cubes, ham cubes.

Vegetables: Small precooked or canned potatoes, tiny cooked or canned onions, baby patty-pan squashes, eggplant crosscuts, quartered green peppers, whole mushrooms, quartered firm-ripe tomatoes, husky slices of cucumber, canned pineapple chunks.

(Dip pepper and mushrooms in boiling water for a minute ahead of time.)

Marinated Lamb Squares

2 envelopes garlic salad-dressing mix
⅔ cup chopped onion
¾ cup chopped celery tips, leaves
⅓ cup vinegar
½ cup salad oil
½ cup cooking sherry
1 tablespoon Worcestershire sauce
2 pounds lamb, in 1½-inch cubes

In deep bowl, combine first 7 ingredients; mix well. Add meat; stir to coat. Refrigerate overnight or let stand at room temperature 2 or 3 hours.

Marinated Beef Cubes

½ cup salad oil
¼ cup vinegar
¼ cup chopped onion
1 teaspoon *each* salt and pepper
2 teaspoons Worcestershire sauce
2 pounds lean beef round or chuck, cut in 1½-inch cubes

In deep bowl, combine first 6 ingredients. Mix well. Add meat; stir to coat. Refrigerate overnight or let stand at room temperature 2 or 3 hours.

Pig-in-a-Poke (*pictured*)

Wrap frankfurter cuts in partially cooked bacon, skewer with folded Bologna slices, dill pickle chunks.

Mandarin Dinner

2 tablespoons butter, melted
¼ cup brown sugar
¼ cup crab-apple syrup
2 teaspoons lemon juice
Canned luncheon meat in 1½-inch cubes
Canned spiced crab apples
Preserved kumquats

Mix first 4 ingredients for glaze; bring to boil. Thread meat, fruits on skewers. Grill slowly; brush often with glaze.

Lunch-on-a-Stick

Thread 1½-inch squares of canned luncheon meat on skewers with quartered orange slices (cut thick, with peel on) and canned sweet potatoes. Broil over slow coals; turn often and brush with Glaze.

Glaze: Combine ½ cup brown sugar, ½ cup orange juice, ¼ cup vinegar, and 1 tablespoon prepared mustard; simmer uncovered 10 minutes.

Armenian Shish Kebab

½ cup olive or salad oil
¼ cup lemon juice
1 teaspoon salt
1 teaspoon marjoram
1 teaspoon thyme
½ teaspoon pepper
1 clove garlic, minced
½ cup chopped onion
¼ cup snipped parsley
2 pounds boneless lamb, cut in
  1½-inch cubes
Green peppers, quartered
Sweet red peppers, quartered
Thick onion slices

In deep bowl, combine first 9 ingredients for herb marinade; mix well. Add meat and stir to coat. Refrigerate overnight or let stand at room temperature 2 or 3 hours, turning meat occasionally.

Fill skewers, alternating meat cubes with chunks of green and red pepper and onion slices. Rotate over hot coals to medium rare, brushing frequently with marinade. Makes 6 servings.

On-a-Saber Beef

Instant meat tenderizer
Round steak, cut in 1½-inch cubes
½ cup extra-hot catsup
2 tablespoons honey
2 tablespoons vinegar
1 tablespoon prepared mustard
2 teaspoons kitchen bouquet
Dash bottled hot pepper sauce

Use tenderizer on meat according to label directions. Skewer meat. Mix remaining ingredients for sauce; brush on meat.

Broil over coals, about 12 to 15 minutes for medium rare, turning frequently and basting often with sauce. Serves 4 or 5.

Abacus Ribs

Little onions, beaded along with the sweet-sour ribs, give recipe its name —

4 pounds spareribs, in narrow strips
1 cup clear French dressing
½ cup finely chopped onion
½ cup chili sauce
2 tablespoons brown sugar
2 to 3 tablespoons lemon juice
2 tablespoons Worcestershire sauce
Cooked or canned small whole onions

Rub ribs with salt and pepper; place in shallow baking dishes. Combine next 6 ingredients for marinade; pour over ribs, coating all. Let stand 2 hours at room temperature or overnight in refrigerator, spooning marinade over occasionally.

Drain, reserving marinade. Lace ribs on spit in accordion style, threading onions on as you weave in and out. Rotate over coals 45 minutes to 1 hour or till not pink when snipped between bones, brushing frequently with marinade. Serves 4.

Mexican Beef Kabobs

As seen on the flowerpot grill buffet, right. Herbs and spices give south-of-the-border flavor —

½ cup chopped onion
1 tablespoon olive oil
1 cup wine vinegar
½ teaspoon salt
½ teaspoon crushed oregano
½ teaspoon cumin
½ teaspoon cloves
½ teaspoon cinnamon
½ teaspoon pepper
1 clove garlic, minced

Instant meat tenderizer
1½ pounds round steak, cut in
  1½-inch cubes

For sauce: Cook onion in hot oil until tender, but not brown. Add vinegar, seasonings, and garlic; cover and simmer 20 minutes; cool.

Meanwhile, use tenderizer on meat according to label directions. Skewer meat; brush with sauce. Broil over hot coals, about 12 to 15 minutes for medium rare, turning frequently and basting often with sauce. Makes 4 or 5 servings.

Sea-food Sword

Two favorite shellfish take on that good soy flavor. Serve with French fries and tomato salad, a fruit-kabob dessert —

¼ cup soy sauce
¼ cup salad oil
¼ cup lemon juice
¼ cup minced parsley
½ teaspoon salt
Dash pepper

• • •

Fresh or frozen shrimp
Fresh or frozen scallops
Large stuffed green olives
Lemon wedges

Combine first 6 ingredients for basting sauce. Peel and devein shrimp, leaving last section of shell and tail intact. Add shrimp and scallops to basting sauce and let stand 1 hour at room temperature, stirring now and then to coat evenly.

On skewers, alternate shrimp*, scallops, olives, and lemon wedges. Broil over hot coals, turning and brushing sea food frequently with the sauce. Don't overcook.

*Efficient lineup: Put shrimp on skewer in pairs, turning the second one upside down and reversing its direction.

Shore Dinner on Kabob

Frozen lobster tails
Fresh or thawed frozen
  shrimp in the shell
Fresh or frozen scallops
Cherry tomatoes
Big stuffed green olives

• • •

Lemon Butter
Tartare Sauce

Partially cook lobster tails by simmering in salted water 10 minutes. With scissors, snip each lobster shell open, remove meat and cut in thirds. Peel and devein shrimp, leaving last section of shell and tail intact. String lobster chunks, shrimp, scallops, tomatoes, and olives on skewers (or use a wiener wheel, if you have one).

Brush with Lemon Butter. Sprinkle with salt. Place on rotisserie. Broil till sea food is done, about 8 to 10 minutes, brushing frequently with Lemon Butter. Before serving, sprinkle with snipped parsley. Serve piping hot with Tartare Sauce.

Lemon Butter: Combine 1 part lemon juice and 2 parts melted butter.

Tartare Sauce: Combine 1 cup mayonnaise, 1 tablespoon minced dill pickle and 1 teaspoon *each* grated onion, minced parsley, and chopped pimiento. Chill.

For fun — flowerpot grills

Line pots to brim with foil; fill ⅔ full of micalike pellets (or use sand or gravel topped with foil). Add 6 or 8 briquets; light. Serve relishes on ice in flowerpots, too.

Grill-side salads, vegetables and breads

Roasted Ears

Corn roasts to caramel-y goodness over hot coals —

Turn back husks and strip off silk. Lay husks back in position. Line ears up on the grill over hot coals. Cook, (keep turning ears) for 15 or 20 minutes, or till husks are dry and browned. (Corn will look sun-tanned. For browner, sweeter corn, continue roasting to suit yourself.)

To serve, break off husks (use glove or towel). Now on with butter, salt, pepper.

Bacon Ears: Turn back husks; remove the silk. Wrap strip of bacon around corn, toothpicking in place. Replace the husks. Roast as above, but when almost done, remove husks and grill to crisp bacon.

Hickory-barbecued Ears: Place corn (in husks) on grill. Add damp hickory to hot coals. Lower hood; cook about 1 hour.

So scrumptious! Try taffy-hued Roasted Ears served steaming hot and dripping with butter. Surprise — bacon crisp-roasted round the cob.

Anise Corn

Perk up corn flavor with sweet spicy aniseed—

Corn on the cob: Husk ears. Place each ear on piece of foil just large enough to lap over $\frac{1}{2}$ inch. Spread corn liberally with soft butter or margarine, sprinkle with salt and dash well with aniseed. Wrap foil loosely around each ear—don't seal seam, but twist ends (so corn will roast instead of steam). Cook corn on grill for 15 to 20 minutes or till tender, turning ears frequently. Offer extra butter, salt, and freshly ground pepper.

Canned corn*: In foilware pan, melt 2 or 3 tablespoons butter or margarine. Drain one 12-ounce or 1-pound can whole kernel corn, and add with $\frac{1}{4}$ teaspoon aniseed. Dash in salt and pepper to taste. Heat, stirring often, till hot.

*For frozen corn, see recipe for Foiled Vegetables; dash well with aniseed.

Foiled Vegetables

Place one block of frozen green beans, peas, or other frozen vegetable on big square of foil. Season with salt and pepper. Top with pat or two of butter.

Bring edges of foil up and, leaving a little space for expansion of steam, seal tightly with double fold. Place package on grill or right in the hot coals about 10 to 15 minutes. Turn occasionally.

Tomatoes in Foil

Onion slices grill 'tween juicy tomato halves—

Cut good, firm tomatoes in half, crosswise. Salt and pepper each half. Put together again with slice of onion between each half, making a "sandwich." Toothpick each tomato together; wrap in foil. Cook away from fire, 35 to 40 minutes.

Grill-top Tomatoes

Cut tomatoes in half. Brush cut surfaces with Italian salad dressing; sprinkle with salt, fresh-ground coarse pepper, and basil. Place cut side up on foil or greased grill over hot coals about 10 minutes or till hot through — don't turn.

Barbecued Rice

Good with grilled burgers — or, add 2 cups diced luncheon meat to foil pouch for meal-in-one —

1⅓ cups packaged precooked rice
½ cup extra-hot catsup
½ cup cold water
1 3-ounce can (⅔ cup) broiled
   sliced mushrooms
¼ cup finely chopped onion
2 tablespoons chopped green pepper
½ teaspoon salt
2 tablespoons butter or margarine

Tear off a 3-foot length of 18-inch-wide foil. Fold in half to make a square. Put fist in center of foil; bring up sides to form pouch. Put all ingredients, except butter, in pouch (mushroom liquid, too). Carefully mix with spoon. Dot with butter. Seal.

Place on grill over hot coals and heat 15 to 18 minutes. Fluff rice with a fork and sprinkle with snipped parsley. Serves 4.

Vegetables on a Spit

Scrub red yams, white turnips, and tart apples (or baking potatoes or acorn squash) — leave all whole in jackets. Wash tomatoes. Core apples. String apples (crosswise) and each kind of vegetable on its own skewer. For tender skins, brush with melted butter or margarine. Let skewers rotate (have hot coals lined up in rows between them). Start yams and apples first — they take 30 to 45 minutes. Allow 25 to 30 minutes for turnips.

Allow 45 minutes to 1 hour for baking potatoes or acorn squash. Tomatoes cook in a jiffy, so start them last of all.

If vegetables get done before the meat (they'll stand still on a rotating spit when done), wrap in foil and lay in firebox away from coals to keep hot.

Skillet Potatoes

Here are fried potatoes with flavor plus —

4 cups cooked potatoes, diced
   (about 6 medium potatoes)
2 cups sliced onions
2 tablespoons snipped parsley
2 tablespoons chopped pimiento
½ teaspoon salt
¼ teaspoon pepper

• • •

¼ cup fat

Combine potatoes, onions, parsley, and pimiento. Add the salt and pepper.

Brown in hot fat in large skillet on top of grill, till golden brown and crisp — keep turning potatoes carefully. Serves 6.

Onioned Potatoes

Open the foil jackets and a tantalizing aroma greets you. These spuds are delicious teamed with burgers or steak —

6 medium baking potatoes
½ cup soft butter or margarine
1 envelope onion-soup mix

Scrub potatoes but do not pare. Cut each in 3 or 4 lengthwise slices. Blend butter and soup mix; spread on slices, then reassemble the potatoes. Wrap each potato in square of foil. overlapping ends.

Bake till done, turning once, on the grill or right on top of coals (takes 45 to 60 minutes). Pass additional butter.

Foiled Spuds

Bake and serve in colored foil — add gaiety to your outdoor barbecues —

Scrub medium baking potatoes (or yams or sweet potatoes). Brush with salad oil. Wrap each potato in a piece of aluminum foil, overlapping ends.

Bake potatoes for 45 to 60 minutes on the grill or right on top of coals. Turn occasionally. Give potatoes the pinch test to tell when they're done.

To serve, cut a crisscross with a fork in the top of each foil package, push on ends to fluff. Top with chunk of butter.

Bake Foiled Potatoes with Parmesan. Dash sparkling Orange Dressing on "just-grilled" steaks for added zing—or, toss with greens.

Flavor tops with barbecued meats—bring out gay Red Onion Relish (the flavor's lemon-tempered) and zesty Calico Potato Salad.

Foiled Potatoes with Parmesan

Scrub 3 large baking potatoes (do not pare). Cut each into ¼-inch lengthwise slices. Spread out on a 20-inch length of 18-inch-wide foil. Dash liberally with onion salt, celery salt, and freshly ground black pepper. Sprinkle with ⅓ cup grated Parmesan cheese. Now overlap potato slices and dot with ⅓ cup butter.

Bring edges of foil together and, leaving a little space for expansion of steam, seal well with a double fold.

Place wrapped potatoes on grill; cook over coals 30 to 45 minutes or till done, turning package several times.

Beanpot

    4 slices bacon
    ½ cup chopped onion
    2 1-pound cans (4 cups) pork and
      beans with tomato sauce
    2 tablespoons brown sugar
    1 to 1½ tablespoons Worcestershire
    1 teaspoon prepared mustard

Cook bacon until crisp; drain, reserving 2 tablespoons drippings. Crumble bacon. Cook onion in reserved drippings till tender but not brown; add with crumbled bacon to remaining ingredients, mixing well. Turn into 1½-quart beanpot or casserole.

Bake the beans uncovered on grill of hickory-smoker, with hood down, about 2 hours. Makes 6 servings.

Pink Beans Supreme

    1 pound (2½ cups) large dry Limas
    2 cups chopped onions
    ½ cup sliced mushrooms
    2 tablespoons paprika
    2 cups dairy sour cream
    1 teaspoon salt

Rinse Limas. Place in pan with 6 cups cold water. Bring to boiling; simmer 2 minutes. Remove from heat. Cover; let stand 1 hour.

Add 2 teaspoons salt to beans (don't drain); place pan on grill, bring to boiling. Move to side of grill; cover, and simmer 45 to 60 minutes or till tender.

In large skillet on grill, cook onions in ¼ cup butter till tender. Add mushrooms, paprika; cook 5 minutes. Stir in beans, sour cream, and salt. Heat. Serves 12.

Red Onion Relish

    3 large red onions, sliced paper-thin
    1 lemon, sliced paper-thin
    ½ cup salad or olive oil
    ¼ cup vinegar
    2 tablespoons lemon juice
    1 teaspoon savory
    ½ teaspoon salt

Layer onion and lemon slices in bowl, ending with lemon. Combine remaining ingredients; pour over. Chill 8 hours; spoon dressing over occasionally. Drain. Makes 2 cups. Good with pork, fish, or burgers.

Orange Dressing

½ cup catsup
½ cup salad oil
2 tablespoons brown sugar
2 tablespoons vinegar
1½ tablespoons prepared mustard
1½ teaspoons Worcestershire sauce
½ teaspoon salt
1 small clove garlic, minced
½ medium orange, unpeeled, cut in
   paper-thin slices and quartered

Combine all ingredients except orange in a quart jar. Cover and shake well. Add orange slices; cover and chill overnight. Brush on steaks as they come off the grill, or toss with greens. Makes about 2 cups.

Calico Potato Salad

5 medium potatoes, cooked and
   sliced (about 5 cups)
2 cups drained cooked cut green beans
1 8-ounce can (1 cup) tiny whole
   beets, drained
½ cup sliced celery
½ cup sliced green onions
½ cup sliced radishes
1 teaspoon salt
½ teaspoon coarse black pepper
• • •
1 cup chilled Horseradish Dressing

Chill the vegetables thoroughly (cut larger beets in half). Combine, and season with salt and pepper. Just before serving, toss vegetable mixture with 1 cup Horseradish Dressing. Makes 8 servings.

Horseradish Dressing: Blend ½ cup mayonnaise or salad dressing, ¼ cup sour cream, and 3 tablespoons prepared horseradish. Add 1 cup clear French dressing, stirring till smooth. Chill. Makes 1¾ cups.

Potluck Potato Salad

6 medium potatoes, cooked in jackets,
   peeled, and cubed (4 cups)
1 onion, chopped
4 hard-cooked eggs, sliced
1 cup chopped celery
1½ teaspoons salt
½ cup salad dressing or mayonnaise

Combine all the ingredients; chill for 4 to 6 hours. Makes 8 servings.

Clear French Dressing

Combine ½ cup salad oil, 2 tablespoons *each* vinegar and lemon juice, 1 teaspoon sugar, ½ teaspoon *each* salt, dry mustard, paprika, and a dash cayenne. Cover; shake well. Makes ¾ cup. Toss with crisp, chilled greens, as pictured below.

Little Caesar Salad

1 clove garlic, minced
¾ cup salad oil
½ head lettuce, chilled
½ bunch curly endive, chilled
1 bunch water cress, chilled
1 uncooked or 1-minute egg
¼ cup lemon juice
1 teaspoon Worcestershire sauce
½ teaspoon salt
¼ teaspoon pepper
3 ounces blue cheese, crumbled
2 cups ¼- to ½-inch croutons

Add garlic to ¼ *cup* salad oil; let stand a few hours. Break greens into bowl. *Combine* ½ *cup* salad oil, egg, lemon juice, Worcestershire sauce, salt, pepper; pour over greens. Add cheese; toss. Pour the garlic salad oil over croutons; toss well. Add to salad; toss lightly. Serves 6.

Salad tossing time. You choose the makings— greens, croutons, French dressing, and various tidbits. For fun, make it right at grill side.

Barbecue Bean Salad

1 1-pound can (2 cups) cut green
   beans, drained
1 1-pound can cut wax beans, drained
1 1-pound can kidney beans, drained
½ cup chopped green pepper

• • •

¾ cup sugar
⅔ cup vinegar
⅓ cup salad oil
1 teaspoon salt
1 teaspoon pepper

Combine vegetables; toss lightly to mix.
Combine sugar, vinegar, and salad oil;
pour over vegetables. Add salt and pepper;
toss lightly. Chill overnight. Before serving,
toss again to coat beans with marinade;
drain. Makes 6 to 8 servings.

Fruited Melon Cups

½ cup dairy sour cream
¼ teaspoon dry mustard
1½ tablespoons honey
½ teaspoon grated orange peel
1 tablespoon orange juice
1 teaspoon lemon juice

• • •

Honeydew melon halves, or slices
Fresh blueberries
Banana slices

Combine sour cream, mustard, and honey.
Beat with electric beater 5 to 7 minutes, or
till fluffy. Add orange peel and dash salt;
slowly beat in fruit juices. Chill at least 1
hour. Makes about ¾ cup.

Fill chilled melon halves with blueberries, banana slices; spoon dressing over.

Spring Coleslaw

2 cups shredded new cabbage
½ cup diced cucumber
½ cup diced celery
¼ cup chopped green pepper
1 teaspoon salt
¼ teaspoon paprika
½ cup salad dressing or mayonnaise
2 tablespoons vinegar
1 teaspoon prepared mustard

Combine chilled vegetables, salt, and paprika. Combine remaining ingredients;
pour over vegetables. Toss. Serves 6.

French Bread with Bar-B-Q Butter

Slash bread on the bias in 1-inch slices,
cutting to, *but not through* the bottom crust.
Blend 2 teaspoons garlic salad-dressing mix
(from envelope) into 1 stick (½ cup) soft
butter. Spread slices. Wrap in foil; heat
bread on grill (turning often).

Grilled Garlic Slices

Melt butter in shallow pan and add
minced garlic. Toast husky slices of French
bread on grill. Then dip both sides into the
garlic butter. Serve bread hot.

Rolls on a Spit

Thread brown-and-serve rolls on a spit.
Brush with melted butter and let rotate
over coals about 10 to 15 minutes.

Barbecue Bread

1 round loaf pumpernickel

• • •

1 stick (½ cup) soft butter
2 tablespoons prepared mustard
½ cup grated Parmesan cheese
¼ cup snipped parsley

Cut bread in ½-inch slices. Mix remaining
ingredients; spread over slices. Put loaf
together on large piece of foil; cut bread
in half lengthwise, going *almost* to bottom
crust. Bring edges of foil over loaf to cover.
Heat at side of grill 20 to 25 minutes or
till hot, turning occasionally. Each person
breaks off his own serving.

Texas Trail Cakes

1 cup packaged biscuit mix
1 6-ounce can evaporated milk
½ of 1-pound can (about ¾ cup)
   canned beans with chili gravy

To biscuit mix, add evaporated milk; beat
smooth. Stir in beans with gravy. Bake on
a hot *well-greased* griddle, (or in a skillet)
on the grill. Turn cakes when top is bubbly and few bubbles have broken; flip only
once. Makes eight 4-inch cakes.

Serve with melted butter (try seasoning
butter with chili powder, if desired).

Easy outdoor desserts

Dessert Kabobs

Cart-wheel Bananas

Leave peel on firm bananas; cut in diagonal slices, about ¾ inch thick. Dip cut ends in lemon juice, then dunk in mixture of brown sugar and cinnamon.

Thread on skewers (going through skin), alternating with quartered orange slices (thick and unpeeled). Broil until hot through and banana peel turns brown.

Candy-Cooky Poles

Alternate big fluffy marshmallows and chocolate drop cookies on a skewer; toast till good and gooey. Turn often.

Cake Kabobs

Cut pound cake or angel cake (from baked goods counter) in 1½-inch cubes. Spear each on fork and dip in melted currant jelly; then roll in flaked coconut to cover. String on skewers and toast over *very hot* coals, turning often.

Or dip cubes of angel or pound cake in sweetened condensed milk, or in a mixture of ½ cup honey and 1 tablespoon lemon juice. Roll in flaked coconut, string on skewers and toast as above.

Fruit-bobs

Thread maraschino cherries in center of canned peach halves—begin and end skewers with halved pineapple ring. Brush with butter and broil, turning often.

Donut Holes

Cut refrigerated biscuits (from a tube) in thirds, and roll each piece into a ball. String on skewers, leaving about ½ inch between balls. "Bake" over *hot* coals, *turning constantly* until browned and completely done, about 7 minutes. At once, push off skewers into melted butter or margarine; roll in cinnamon-sugar mixture. Eat right away! One tube makes 30 "donuts."

Cookout finale—whirling dessert kabobs served piping hot off the skewer! Choose from our array, or have fun trying your own.

Pineapple-on-a-Spit

Pare a medium pineapple, leaving leafy crown intact. Remove eyes and, if desired, replace with 15 to 20 whole cloves. Center pineapple on spit—you may need to pull out a few spikes from center and "blaze the trail" with a small skewer. Secure with holding fork. Wrap leafy end in foil.

Let rotate over hot coals 45 minutes to 1 hour, basting frequently with mixture of ½ cup maple-flavored syrup and ½ teaspoon cinnamon. Slice and serve hot.

Hickory Nuts

Brush fresh pecan meats, peanuts, or almonds with butter. Salt, and place on sheet of foil. Hickory-smoke for 20 minutes.

Hot Banana Shortcake

¼ cup butter or margarine
2 or 3 green-tipped bananas,
    peeled and quartered
2 tablespoons lemon juice
⅔ cup brown sugar
¼ teaspoon cinnamon
4 1-inch slices pound cake
Vanilla ice cream or
    dairy sour cream

Melt butter in foilware pan over hot coals. Add bananas, drizzle with lemon juice, and sprinkle with brown sugar and cinnamon. Cook until bananas are just soft, spooning the syrup over now and then.

Meanwhile, on the grill, toast cake slices on both sides. To serve, spoon bananas and syrup over the warm cake slices. Top with scoops of vanilla ice cream or dollops of sour cream. Makes 4 servings.

Strawberry Ice Cream

1 quart strawberries, washed,
    drained and hulled
½ to ⅔ cup sugar
• • •
1 cup sugar
2 tablespoons all-purpose flour
Dash salt
1½ cups milk
2 beaten eggs
2 cups whipping cream
1 teaspoon vanilla

Sprinkle strawberries with ½ to ⅔ cup sugar, depending on sweetness of berries; mash; chill. Mix 1 cup sugar, flour, and salt; stir in milk. Cook and stir over low heat till mixture thickens. Stir small amount of hot mixture into eggs; then add the eggs to hot mixture. Cook, stirring constantly for 1 minute. Chill.

To custard add mashed berries, cream and vanilla. Freeze in 2-quart (or larger) ice-cream freezer, using 6 parts ice to 1 part salt. Being careful not to get brine in ice cream, remove dasher. Plug opening in lid; cover can with several thicknesses of waxed paper or foil for tight fit; replace lid. Pack more ice and salt (use 4 parts ice to 1 part salt) around can to fill freezer. Cover freezer with heavy cloth or newspapers. Let ripen about 4 hours. Makes 1½ quarts.

Powwow Sundae

¼ pound (about 16)
    large marshmallows
1 cup canned chocolate syrup
Vanilla ice cream

String marshmallows on skewers. Toast over coals till melty inside and well-browned outside (best of all if marshmallows blaze a little to get crackly edges!).

Scoot hot, gooey-good marshmallows off skewers into a serving bowl of chocolate sauce. Stir just to marble. To make sundaes, ladle sauce over big scoops of vanilla ice cream. Makes 1½ cups sauce.

Melon-patch Treats

Choose juicy, ripe melons; chill icy-cold. Cut generous thumping-ripe watermelon wedges; be sure to pass the salt shaker for those who like a dash.

Or, serve a tray with three kinds of melon — watermelon, cantaloupe, honeydew — and lime wedges for zip. Another grill-side dessert: Squirt a lineup of chilled cantaloupe sections with lemon juice, tuck in clusters of juicy dark grapes.

Dessert time is easy with these

Kids'll love S'mores. Just sandwich gooey, toasted marshmallows and a milk chocolate square 'tween 2 graham crackers and squish!

Melon-ball Refresher

Cool, cool—tumble gay melon balls into frosty glasses, cascade bubbly ginger ale over all—

Rub parfait glasses with fresh mint and chill. Then fill with chilled watermelon, cantaloupe, and honeydew melon balls. Add a bit of lemon juice and top with mint sprig. Pass pitcher of chilled ginger ale to pour over balls—adds tasty zing.

Grill-baked Pudding Cake

Dessert bakes atop grill while you eat dinner —

Prepare 1 package pudding-cake mix (use your favorite flavor) according to package directions, but using an ungreased 8½x1½-inch round foilware pan. (Wait till you are ready to bake the cake before preparing the mix.)

Place on grill top over hot coals; lower hood to make oven. Bake cake for about 25 to 30 minutes or till done.

Spoon out servings while warm, turning each one pudding-side up. Extra good topped with scoop of vanilla ice cream.

Roll-'n-fruit Dessert Bobs

Sweet rolls and fruit tidbits toast side by side—

Fold 1 yard heavy-duty aluminum foil in half; grease top. Open 1 tube of refrigerated cinnamon rolls; arrange rolls near one end of foil. Fold other end of foil over and pinch edges together—allow about ½ inch in package, above rolls, for rising. Place package about 8 inches above hot coals; bake 7 minutes or so—peek now and then to see if bottoms of rolls are brown. Invert; bake about 7 minutes longer.

Meanwhile, mix icing that comes in cinnamon-roll package with 1 tablespoon pineapple or apricot syrup; set aside.

Cut or snip each baked roll in thirds. Fill the skewers, alternating pieces of baked roll with marshmallows, canned pineapple chunks, maraschino cherries, canned apricot halves, cooked pitted prunes, and spiced crab apples.

Roast the kabobs over hot coals, turning skewers often, till sweet rolls and marshmallows are toasted. With a fork scoot the hot foods off skewers and drizzle icing mixture over all. Eat at once!

Make ice cream balls early; freeze and serve in same foil pan. Offer toppings in foil pans, too. Bonus: no dishes to do—just toss 'em.

A party quickie! Tempting towers of fruit and ice cream molded in pretty paper cups. Fix ahead and freeze—unmold or serve as is.

Extra-special extras– appetizers and relishes

Hot appetizer kabobs keep guests happy till dinner's on. Try roasting Mushroom Buttons, Bacon-Cheese Bites, Cocktail Totem, Western Starter, or Shrimpkin—simply delicious

Mushroom Buttons

Wash fresh mushrooms (don't soak or peel), or use large canned mushroom crowns. Remove stems. Fill mushroom crowns generously with canned deviled ham; put two together to make sandwiches. Alternate mushroom "sandwiches" on skewers with pickled onions.

Brush with melted butter or margarine. Rotate over coals about 4 to 5 minutes or till mushrooms are done, brushing frequently with the melted butter.

Bacon-Cheese Bites

Wrap 1-inch cubes of sharp process American cheese in partially cooked slices of bacon. Rotate the wrapped cheese cubes over coals, till bacon is done and cheese is melty—takes just a few minutes.

Olives-in-Bacon Appetizers

Wrap large stuffed olives with bacon strips and pin with toothpick. Place olives on a sheet of foil and hickory-smoke away from fire for about 35 minutes.

Western Starter

Gives your patio dinner a touch of sophistication—

Let canned artichoke hearts stand in Italian salad dressing for several hours. Slice canned water chestnuts in thirds. Cut chicken livers in slices slightly larger than the chestnut slices; dip in soy sauce.

Sandwich a piece of chestnut between two slices of chicken liver; wrap with a half-slice of bacon and fasten with toothpick. Alternate bacon-wrapped chicken livers and artichoke hearts on skewers.

Rotate the appetizers over hot coals for about 7 minutes or till chicken livers are done and bacon is crisp. Serve hot.

Cocktail Totems

2 tablespoons instant minced onion
¼ cup evaporated milk
1 egg
½ pound ground beef
½ cup fine cracker crumbs
½ teaspoon salt
3 dashes bottled hot pepper sauce
Canned or packaged cocktail franks
Large stuffed green olives

• • •

¼ cup butter or margarine, melted
Dash liquid smoke

For meat balls: soak instant onion in evaporated milk a few minutes. Thoroughly combine meat and egg; add crumbs, milk, salt, and pepper sauce, mixing well. Shape in 1-inch balls (makes about 16).

For totem-pole effect, fill skewers in this order: meat ball, 2 cocktail franks (threaded crosswise), stuffed olive.

Combine butter and liquid smoke and brush on kabobs. Rotate over hot coals about 5 minutes or till meat balls are done, brushing frequently with smoke-butter.

Shrimpkin

¾ cup chopped onion
½ cup salad oil
¾ cup catsup
¾ cup water
⅓ cup lemon juice
3 tablespoons sugar
3 tablespoons Worcestershire sauce
2 tablespoons prepared mustard
2 teaspoons salt
¼ teaspoon bottled hot pepper sauce
Fresh or frozen shrimp

For sauce, cook onion in the oil till tender, but not brown. Add next 8 ingredients; simmer uncovered 15 minutes. Peel and devein shrimp; leave last section of shell and tail intact. Brush with sauce. Rotate over hot coals till shrimp are done, 5 to 8 minutes; brush often with sauce. Pass bowl of remaining sauce. Makes 2½ cups.

Hot Chop-Chop

Combine ½ cup *each* chopped green pepper, chopped· onion, and chili sauce. Chill, if desired. Makes 1¼ cups relish.

Pepper Pups

1 pound (8 to 10) frankfurters
2 tablespoons butter or margarine
1 teaspoon coarse cracked pepper
1 teaspoon marjoram

Slice franks in bite-size pieces. Melt butter with seasonings in foil pan. Add franks and brown, turning often (have coals hot-hot). Spear with toothpicks—folks help themselves. Serves 10 to 12.

Appetizer Ham Kabobs

Spread thin boiled ham slices lightly with prepared mustard. Fold each slice in thirds, then cut in half or thirds (bite-size pieces). String the ham fold-ups on skewers, alternating with stuffed green olives and cooked or canned small whole onions.

Brush all with bottled Italian salad dressing. Broil over hot coals, about 5 minutes or till barbecue-y, turning and brushing frequently with the dressing.

Broiled Banana Appetizers

Choose yellow bananas with green tips —not too ripe. Peel; wrap bacon strip around each and peg with toothpick (don't let ends of picks stick out).

With pancake turner roll bananas back and forth on greased grill top until bacon is cooked, about 5 minutes. (Takes a hot fire—you want bacon to crisp before banana cooks too much.) Count on a small banana or half a large one per serving.

Gosh and Golly Relish

2 medium tomatoes, finely
    chopped and drained well
1 medium onion, finely chopped
1 small green pepper, finely chopped
3 or 4 small hot pickled Italian
    peppers, chopped (1 tablespoon)
2 tablespoons sugar
½ teaspoon mustard seed
½ teaspoon celery seed
½ teaspoon salt
¼ cup white vinegar

Combine ingredients except vinegar; cover with vinegar. Chill well. Makes 2 cups.

Real cool cooking

When the temperature soars, it's
time for line-of-least-resistance
meals. Call on sandwich suppers,
salad-plate refreshers, and
porch picnics, to keep family and
guests happy and well-fed,
you a carefree summertime cook!

Take your choice of hot and cold foods

← Stack up a Walking Sandwich—fork a slice of corned beef
atop Swiss cheese on rye, and, if you like, add a mound of
Summer Slaw. With baked beans, fruit, tea—it's a meal.

Or choose old-favorite Perfect Fried Chicken and pair
with quickie go-withs. For a cooling make-ahead meal, offer
a salad trio—Tuna Mousse, Garden Perfection Loaf, honeydew wedges topped off with fresh strawberries. Pass little hot
breads—Mexican Swirls, Cheese Wedges—plus dessert, tea.

Patio sandwich suppers

When the temperature soars and cooking's out of the question, it's sandwich time. Stock up on interesting breads, table-ready meats, a variety of cheese—you can put a meal together in no time at all. Don't forget paper plates and throw-away forks.

```
.....................................
.                                   .
.    Buffet-Sandwich Special        .
.                                   .
.        Walking Sandwich           .
.     Mustard     Dill Pickles      .
.       Saucy Baked Beans           .
.         Ginger Peachy             .
.            Iced Tea               .
.                                   .
.....................................
```

Walking Sandwich

    12 slices rye bread, buttered
    6 slices Swiss cheese
    12 thin slices cooked corned
      beef, chilled
    1 recipe Summer Slaw

For each sandwich, fill between slices of rye with Swiss cheese, 2 slices corned beef, and Summer Slaw. Makes 6 servings.

Summer Slaw

    1 tablespoon prepared mustard
    ½ cup salad dressing
    3 tablespoons light cream or top milk
    2 tablespoons vinegar
    2 tablespoons finely chopped onion
    ¼ teaspoon caraway seed
    3 cups *finely* shredded cabbage

Stir mustard into salad dressing. Add cream and vinegar. Toss onion and caraway seed with chilled cabbage; add only enough of the dressing to moisten, then toss. Pass remaining dressing with Walking Sandwich. Makes 6 servings as sandwich topper, 4 to 5 servings as salad.

Saucy Baked Beans

Bake these in the morning while it's cool—

    6 slices bacon, cut in
      1-inch pieces
            •   •   •
    3 1-pound cans (6 cups) baked beans
      in pork and molasses sauce
            •   •   •
    1 8-ounce can (1 cup) seasoned
      tomato sauce
    1 cup chopped onion
    ½ cup catsup
    ¼ cup brown sugar
    2 tablespoons prepared mustard
    1 teaspoon salt
    4 drops bottled hot
      pepper sauce

Cook bacon till almost crisp; drain. Combine bacon and beans; add tomato sauce, onion, catsup, brown sugar, mustard, salt, and bottled hot pepper sauce.

Bake beans, uncovered, in 2-quart casserole or beanpot in slow oven (300°) for 3 to 5 hours. Makes 6 servings.

Ginger Peachy

Another time, serve fruit mixture alone—

    4 cups sliced fresh peaches*
    ½ cup orange juice
    3 tablespoons honey
    2 tablespoons finely chopped
      candied ginger
    Dash salt
            •   •   •
    Vanilla ice cream

Combine peaches, orange juice, honey, ginger, and salt; mix gently. Cover; chill thoroughly. To serve, spoon over vanilla ice cream. Makes 5 or 6 servings.

*To keep golden peach color, brush cut fruit with a little lemon juice. Or, you can use the ascorbic-acid mixture you add when freezing light-colored fruits; follow label directions for fresh cut fruit.

Dutch Lunch

Sliced Cold Cuts, Luncheon Meat
Sliced Cheese, Onions
Rye Bread
Pepped-up Potato Salad
Herbed Tomatoes   Deviled Eggs
Ruby Fruit Compote, *or*
Pears a la Compote
Coffee

Deviled Eggs

Halve 6 hard-cooked eggs lengthwise; remove yolks. Mash yolks; mix with ¼ cup mayonnaise or salad dressing, 1 teaspoon vinegar, 1 teaspoon prepared mustard, ½ teaspoon salt, and dash pepper. Refill egg whites, using pastry tube, if desired. Chill. Trim with thin pimiento strips.

Sour-cream Potato Salad

7 medium potatoes, cooked in jacket, peeled and sliced (6 cups)
⅓ cup clear French or Italian dressing
¾ cup sliced celery
⅓ cup sliced green onions and tops
4 hard-cooked eggs
1 cup mayonnaise
½ cup dairy sour cream
1½ teaspoons prepared horseradish mustard
Salt and celery seed to taste
⅓ cup diced pared cucumber

While potatoes are warm, pour dressing over and then chill for 2 hours.

Add celery and onion. Chop egg whites; add. Sieve yolks; reserve some for garnish. Combine remaining sieved yolk with mayonnaise, sour cream, and horseradish mustard. Fold into salad. Add salt and celery seed to taste. Chill salad for 2 hours. Add diced cucumber; mix.

To trim, sprinkle reserved sieved yolk and sliced onion tops over top. Serves 8.

Easy Dutch Lunch—just set out the makings and say help yourself

No fuss with this meal—you set it up buffet-style and invite guests to serve themselves. They circle round and build their own sandwiches as they go—it's fun!

Herbed Tomatoes

    6 ripe tomatoes, peeled
    1 teaspoon salt
    ¼ teaspoon coarse black pepper
    Few leaves fresh thyme or marjoram,
       or ½ teaspoon of dried
    ¼ cup finely snipped parsley
    ¼ cup snipped chives
    ⅔ cup salad oil
    ¼ cup tarragon vinegar

Place tomatoes in bowl; sprinkle with seasonings and herbs. Combine oil and vinegar; pour over. Cover; chill one hour; occasionally spoon dressing over. To serve, drain dressing to pass in bowl; arrange tomatoes in serving dish. Snip additional parsley or chives over. Makes 6 servings.

Ruby Fruit Compote

    1 No. 2 can (2½ cups) frozen pitted
       tart red cherries, thawed
    1 10-ounce package frozen
       raspberries, thawed
    1½ tablespoons cornstarch
    1 tablespoon lemon juice
    2 cups fresh whole strawberries
    Dairy sour cream

Drain frozen fruits, reserving syrup. Add water to syrup to measure 2½ cups. Blend cornstarch, dash salt, and the syrup. Cook and stir till thick and clear. Add lemon juice. Stir in fruits. Sweeten, if desired. Chill thoroughly. Spoon into sherbets; top with sour cream. Makes 8 servings.

Pears a la Compote

    1 cup sugar
    3 cups water
    ⅓ cup lime or lemon juice
    Dash salt
    4 fresh pears
    2 cups seeded Tokay or Emperor grapes
    Dash aromatic bitters

Combine first 4 ingredients; heat to boiling. Meanwhile, halve pears lengthwise, leaving stem intact, and core (don't pare); add to syrup. Cover; cook 20 minutes or till tender. Arrange grapes and pears in dish. Add bitters to syrup to taste. Pour syrup over fruits; chill. Serves 8.

> ### Soup 'n Sandwiches
>
> Choice of Chilled Soups
> (Tomato Cooler, Easy Vichyssoise,
> Jellied Consomme)
> Broiled Cheese Sandwiches
> Strawberry Parfait Pie

Tomato Cooler

Thoroughly combine 1 can condensed tomato soup, 1 cup light cream, ½ teaspoon nutmeg, and ¼ teaspoon salt. Blend or shake till smooth. Chill. Serves 4 or 5.

Easy Vichyssoise

Heat 1 can frozen condensed cream of potato soup to thaw; add 1 can condensed cream of chicken soup and 1 can milk. Beat, or blend in blender. Add 1 cup light cream. Cover; chill. Snip chives atop. Serves 5.

Jellied Consomme

Chill 2 cans of consomme for 3 hours in refrigerator (or 1 hour in freezer). Serve with lemon wedges. Makes 5 or 6 servings.

Luscious, light, and chock full of fresh sweet berries—Strawberry Parfait Pie is perfect finale for a summer luncheon. Pass hot coffee.

It's Soup 'n Sandwiches

But, there's a switch—here the soups are served icy-*cold* and the sandwiches come melting-*hot* off the broiler. This new combo is great for warm days—the family'll love it.

Lattice Cheese Sandwiches

6 slices bread

. . .

1 2¼-ounce can deviled ham
6 slices sharp process cheese, cut
in 1½x3-inch strips

Toast bread and trim crusts. Butter on one side lightly, then spread with deviled ham. Top ham with lattice of cheese strips. Broil 3 inches from heat just till cheese *starts* to melt. Makes 6 sandwiches.

Bacon 'n Tomato Special

6 slices bacon, halved

. . .

6 slices bread
6 or 12 tomato slices
1 cup shredded sharp
process American cheese

Broil bacon till crisp. Toast bread; trim crusts and butter on one side lightly.

Place 2 pieces of bacon on buttered side of toast; top with 1 or 2 tomato slices and shredded cheese. Broil sandwiches 3 inches from heat just till cheese begins to melt. Makes 6 sandwiches.

Strawberry Parfait Pie

1½ cups sifted all-purpose flour
½ teaspoon salt
½ cup shortening
4 to 5 tablespoons cold water

. . .

1 3-ounce package strawberry-
flavored gelatin
1 cup hot water
½ cup cold water
1 pint vanilla ice cream
1 cup sliced fresh strawberries

. . .

Whipping cream, whipped
Whole ripe berries for trim

Prepare pastry from first 4 ingredients. Line 9-inch pie plate, prick; bake at 450° for 10 to 12 minutes; cool.

Meanwhile, dissolve gelatin in hot water; add ½ cup cold water and stir. Cut ice cream into 6 chunks and add to gelatin; stir till ice cream melts. Chill till mixture mounds slightly when spooned (20 to 30 minutes). Gently fold in sliced berries. Pour into cooled pastry shell; chill several hours or till firm.

Trim with whipped cream and berries (split from the tip almost through).

Salad-plate refreshers

Aloha!

Hawaiian Chicken Salad
Banana Bread
Kona Coffee Torte
Hilo Punch or Iced Coffee

Inspiration Island-style Lush fresh pineapple and hibiscus blossoms add a party air to Hawaiian Chicken Salad. If you're feeling *really* fancy, thread flower petals on beverage stirrers, too!

Hawaiian Chicken Salad

2 large oranges
2 fresh pineapples
3 cups diced cooked or
   canned chicken
1 cup chopped celery
½ cup toasted slivered almonds
Dressing:
1 cup mayonnaise or salad dressing
½ teaspoon salt
¼ teaspoon marjoram

Have all ingredients chilled. Section oranges, reserving 2 tablespoons juice for dressing. Reserve 4 orange sections for garnish; dice remaining orange.

Cut each pineapple in half lengthwise, through leafy top and all. Cut a 1-inch-thick lengthwise slice off each half, to make 4 slices complete with leafy tops. Cut off lower third of each slice. Pare and core cut-off pieces and remaining unsliced pineapple; cut into chunks.

For salad, mix diced orange sections, 1 cup pineapple chunks, chicken, celery, and almonds. For dressing, blend mayonnaise, 2 tablespoons reserved orange juice, salt, and marjoram; toss with salad. Place two pineapple slices end to end and pile high with half the salad mixture.

Garnish with orange sections. If you wish, add fresh strawberries, pink grapefruit sections, and honeydew melon balls, as well. Repeat with remaining salad and pineapple. Makes 6 servings.

Banana Bread

⅓ cup shortening
½ cup sugar
2 eggs
1¾ cups sifted all-purpose flour
1 teaspoon baking powder
½ teaspoon *each* soda and salt
1 cup mashed ripe banana
   (2 to 3 bananas)
½ cup chopped California walnuts

Cream together shortening and sugar; add eggs and beat well. Sift together dry ingredients; add to creamed mixture alternately with banana, blending well after each addition. Stir in walnuts. Pour into a well-greased 9½x5x3-inch loaf pan. Bake at 350° for 40 to 45 minutes or till done. Remove from pan; cool on rack.

Kona Coffee Torte
(*From Kona Inn, Hawaii*)

1½ tablespoons instant coffee powder
1 cup cold water
6 egg yolks
2 cups sugar
2 cups sifted all-purpose flour
3 teaspoons baking powder
¼ teaspoon salt
1 teaspoon vanilla
1 cup ground walnuts
6 stiff-beaten egg whites

Dissolve coffee in water. Beat egg yolks until light and fluffy; gradually add sugar, beating until thick. Sift together dry ingredients; add to creamed mixture alternately with coffee, beating after each addition. Add vanilla and ground walnuts. Fold in stiff-beaten egg whites.

Bake in 3 paper-lined 9x1½-inch round pans in slow oven (325°) about 30 minutes or till done. Fill cooled cake with Orange Filling; frost with Mocha Frosting. Garnish with California walnut halves.

Orange Filling

Cream 1 cup butter; gradually add 2 cups sifted confectioners' sugar, creaming well. Beat in 2 teaspoons dry cocoa, ½ teaspoon instant coffee, 2 tablespoons cold water and 2 tablespoons orange juice.

Mocha Frosting

Mix 2 cups sifted confectioners' sugar, 2 teaspoons dry cocoa, and ½ teaspoon instant coffee; add 2 tablespoons cold water, 3 tablespoons melted butter and ½ teaspoon vanilla. Beat to spreading consistency.

Hilo Punch

Combine ⅓ cup sugar, ⅓ cup water, 8 whole cloves and 4 inches stick cinnamon in saucepan; simmer covered 5 minutes. Cool; strain, combining with 3 cups canned pineapple-orange-juice drink and ⅓ cup lemon juice. Chill.

At serving time, add 2 teaspoons rum flavoring and pour over ice cubes in punch bowl or pitcher; last minute pour one small bottle chilled ginger ale carefully down side. Makes about 1 quart.

Salad Buffet

Garden Perfection Loaf
Tuna Mousse
Honeydew Wedges
with Strawberries
Mexican Swirls   Cheese Wedges
Lemon Angel Frost *or*
Tropical Sundaes
Hot Tea

Perfection Salad

2 envelopes (2 tablespoons)
   unflavored gelatin
½ cup sugar
1 teaspoon salt
1½ cups boiling water
1½ cups cold water
½ cup vinegar
2 tablespoons lemon juice

• • •

2 cups *finely* shredded cabbage
1 cup chopped celery
¼ cup chopped green pepper
¼ cup diced pimiento
⅓ cup stuffed green-olive slices

Thoroughly mix the gelatin, sugar, and salt. Add boiling water and stir to dissolve the gelatin. Then add cold water, vinegar, and lemon juice. Chill till partially set.

Add remaining ingredients. Pour into an 8½x4½x2½-inch loaf pan. Chill till firm.

Just before mealtime, unmold and garnish salad with carrot curls and ripe olives.

Garden Perfection Loaf (as shown on page 38): Prepare the *gelatin* mixture as in the above recipe, but *do not chill.*

Combine 1 cup *finely* shredded cabbage and 2 tablespoons chopped pimiento in an 8½x4½x2½-inch loaf pan. Pour *1 cup* of the gelatin mixture over; chill till *almost* set. Meanwhile, chill remaining gelatin till partially set. Combine 1 cup *thinly* sliced carrot rounds with 1 cup of the partially set gelatin. Pour over first layer; chill till *almost* set. Combine remaining gelatin with 1 cup drained cooked or canned peas. Pour over carrot layer. Chill till firm. Unmold. Garnish. Makes 6 to 8 servings.

Add the boiling water to the gelatin. Stir until all gelatin is thoroughly dissolved.

Add cabbage, green pepper, pimiento, green-olive slices, celery to the gelatin mixture.

Unmold your salad on a chilled platter. Garnish with carrot curls, ripe olives, romaine.

Tuna Mousse

A beautiful salad loaf for the mainstay of a cool lunch or supper —

1½ tablespoons (1½ envelopes) unflavored gelatin
½ cup cold water
¼ cup lemon juice
. . .
1 cup mayonnaise
2 6½- or 7-ounce cans (2 cups) tuna, coarsely flaked
½ cup chopped pared cucumber
½ cup thinly sliced celery
¼ cup sliced stuffed green olives
2 teaspoons onion juice
1½ teaspoons prepared horseradish
¼ teaspoon salt
¼ teaspoon paprika
1 cup whipping cream, whipped

Soften gelatin in cold water in saucepan. Add lemon juice. Heat and stir over medium heat till gelatin is dissolved. Stir into mayonnaise. Add tuna and remaining ingredients except cream. Mix well; fold in whipped cream. Pour into an 8½x4½x 2½-inch loaf pan. Chill till firm. Unmold; serve with lime wedges. Serves 8.

Mexican Swirls

1 package hot-roll mix
. . .
1 slightly beaten egg
½ teaspoon salt
½ teaspoon celery seed
2 tablespoons chopped pimiento
2 cups shredded sharp process American cheese
Dash coarse black pepper

Prepare dough and let rise as directed on the hot-roll-mix package. Meanwhile, combine remaining ingredients. Divide dough into two parts. On lightly floured surface, roll each to a 12x9-inch rectangle.

Spread dough with filling. Starting at long side, roll each up as for jellyroll. Seal edges. Cut in 1-inch slices. Place cut side down in well-greased muffin cups (about 2¾-inch diameter).

Cover; let rise till almost double (30 to 40 minutes). Bake in hot oven (400°) 15 minutes or till done. Makes about 2 dozen Mexican Swirls.

Cheese Wedges

1 well-beaten egg
½ cup milk
1½ cups packaged biscuit mix
1 cup grated sharp process American cheese
2 teaspoons poppy seed
2 tablespoons butter or margarine, melted

Combine egg and milk; add to biscuit mix and stir only till dry ingredients are just moistened. Add half the cheese. Spread dough in greased 8x1½-inch round baking dish. Sprinkle with remaining cheese and the poppy seed; drizzle melted butter over all. Bake at 400° about 20 minutes. Cut in wedges and serve hot. Serves 6 to 8.

Lemon Angel Frost

2 egg whites
½ cup sugar
. . .
2 egg yolks
½ teaspoon grated lemon peel
¼ cup lemon juice
½ cup whipping cream, whipped
Semisweet-chocolate curls

Beat egg whites till soft peaks form; gradually add sugar, beating to stiff peaks. Beat egg yolks till thick and lemon colored. Fold egg yolks, lemon peel, and lemon juice into egg whites. Fold in whipped cream. Pour into refrigerator tray; freeze firm. Serve in sherbets. Top with shaved semisweet chocolate. Serves 6 to 8.

Tropical Sundaes

3 tablespoons mashed ripe banana
1½ teaspoons lemon juice
½ cup orange marmalade
½ cup pineapple-apricot preserves
Rum flavoring to taste
Vanilla ice cream
½ cup flaked coconut, toasted

Combine banana and lemon juice; add marmalade and preserves. Cook 5 minutes over low heat, stirring constantly. Remove from heat; stir in rum flavoring. Makes about 1⅓ cups. Spoon warm sauce over ice cream. Top with the toasted coconut.

Ideal for summertime

It's delicious and it's fast (everything's quick to fix or cook). Borrow an idea from drive-ins—serve in individual baskets, ready to "take out" to porch or back yard.

Have a porch picnic

Chicken Basket Dinner

Perfect Fried Chicken
Potato Patties
Corn Coblets
Tomato Salad Mold
Parsley-butter Loaf
Peach Shortcake Dessert Cups
Hot Coffee or Iced Tea

Parsley-butter Loaf

1 1-pound loaf unsliced sandwich bread
½ cup soft butter
½ cup chopped parsley
1 tablespoon lemon juice

Trim crust from top and sides of bread. Cut loaf in half lengthwise, *almost* to bottom crust. Then cut crosswise in 12 slices, *almost* to bottom. Combine remaining ingredients; spread between slices.

Bake on cooky sheet at 375° for 8 to 10 minutes, or till hot. Sprinkle with parsley.

Perfect Fried Chicken

¾ cup all-purpose flour
1 tablespoon salt
1 tablespoon paprika
¼ teaspoon pepper

• • •

1 2½- to 3-pound ready-to-cook
   broiler-fryer, cut up

Combine flour and seasonings in paper or plastic bag; add 2 or 3 pieces of chicken at a time and shake. Place on rack to let coating dry. Heat fat (¼ inch deep in skillet) till it will sizzle a drop of water.

Brown meaty pieces first; then slip others in. Brown one side; turn with tongs. When lightly browned, 15 to 20 minutes, reduce heat; cover tightly. (If cover isn't tight, add 1 tablespoon water.) Cook until tender, 30 to 40 minutes. Uncover last 10 minutes to crisp. Makes 4 servings.

Potato Patties

Combine 2 cups leftover mashed potatoes, 1 beaten egg, and ¼ cup chopped onion; season with salt and pepper; mix well. Shape 6 patties; dip in flour. Brown slowly in butter, about 5 minutes on each side. Makes 6 servings.

For speed: Fry frozen patties.

Corn Coblets

Remove husks from fresh corn. Remove silks with stiff brush. Rinse. Break ears in half. Cook covered in small amount of boiling salted water or uncovered in boiling salted water to cover 6 to 8 minutes.

Tomato Salad Mold

1 3-ounce package lemon-flavored
   gelatin
1¼ cups hot water
1 8-ounce can seasoned tomato sauce
1½ tablespoons vinegar
½ teaspoon salt
Dash pepper

Dissolve gelatin in hot water. Blend in remaining ingredients. Pour into 3-cup mold or individual molds. Chill till firm.

Unmold on lettuce. Add garnish of relishes: carrot curls, cucumber cuts, and green-pepper strips. Makes 5 servings.

Peach Shortcake Dessert Cups

Fill sponge cake dessert cups (from a package) with sweetened whipped cream. Top with chilled canned peach halves, hollow side up. Center with dollop of whipped cream. Pass extra sliced peaches.

Fruit—perfect ending—

Whip up double-decker Peach Shortcake Dessert Cups just before serving — they take only a minute. (If you wish, dash nutmeg atop.) And don't forget steaming coffee.

Meals on the go!

These easy-traveling meals dress to fit the occasion. Whether it's casual for beach, tailored to boat or car trips, hobo-style for the kids, or elegant for a lawn supper, there's carefree picnicking ahead!

Here's a first-rate picnic idea

← Pack the lunch in the back of the station wagon—at the picnic spot, just set everything up on the tailgate and let picnickers help themselves. It's an outdoor buffet!

Cook-a-little picnics

It's fresh air and sunshine when picnic weather rolls around. A velvety lawn, trip to the beach, walk through the woods, or a fabulous 2-week vacation, *all* call for grand, carefree picnicking. Don't forget Dad when he goes fishing, or the kids on their bike rides—perfect time for picnic lunches. Whether you go as far as the mountains, or as near as the back yard, you can make any day a vacation—just fill the picnic basket, grab an old blanket, and head for the great out of doors!

If you're traveling far, these foods can be taken safely without refrigeration:
• Canned foods—meats, fruit and fruit juices, vegetables (like the old picnic favorite, baked beans), and others.
• Process cheese
• Watermelon, cantaloupe, apples, oranges, bananas, and other fresh fruits
• Tomatoes
• Potato chips, crackers
• Cookies, cake (but *no* cream fillings), fruit pies (again, no cream fillings)
• Doughnuts
• Jelly, jam, and peanut butter
• Hard-cooked eggs (for one day only)

In-a-minute Steaks

½ teaspoon instant minced onion
3 tablespoons wine vinegar
½ cup salad oil
1 teaspoon seasoned salt
Dash freshly ground pepper
2 teaspoons Worcestershire sauce
6 cube steaks
6 slices sharp process American cheese
6 hamburger buns, toasted, buttered

Soak onion in vinegar few minutes; add oil and seasonings, mixing well. Place meat in container; pour marinade over, coating well. Cover; let stand an hour or so—spoon marinade once or twice and keep cool. Grill over very hot coals about 2 minutes per side. Last minute lay cheese slices atop each steak. Serve on hot buns. Serves 6.

Olive Dressing

Soften ½ of a 3-ounce package cream cheese. Gradually add 1 cup Italian or clear French dressing, beating smooth. Stir in ¼ teaspoon paprika and ⅓ cup chopped stuffed green olives. Makes 1⅓ cups.

Tailgate Feast

In-a-minute Steaks, Grilled Franks
Hamburger Buns, Coney Rolls
Catsup   Mustard
Pickles and Relishes
Green Salad with Olive Dressing
Watermelon Wedges
Hot Coffee, Bottled Drinks

Flip the station wagon tailgate down —it's a built-in buffet! Everyone chefs his own meat, then helps himself to the picnic array. Hint: Melon rides uncut in crushed ice till all's ready.

Sand-and-Surf Special

Grilled Steaks*   Roasted Ears*
Relish Salad
Parmesan Dressing Italiano
French Bread to Toast
Cantaloupe   Hawaiian Lemonade

It's a beach party! After a day's swim, start the steaks sizzling and unpack the basket. Then, build up a blazing fire to light your supper and to sing around as the stars come out. Food tastes great, sand and all!
*See index listing

Sand-and-Surf Special

Supper by firelight—happy finale to a day at the beach. Eat hearty of juicy steaks, golden roasting ears, and salad. For dessert surprise: Serve cantaloupe alamode.

Relish Salad

Arrange tomato slices, green pepper rings, cucumber slices, and cauliflowerets on crisp lettuce leaves; pour Parmesan Dressing Italiano over.

Parmesan Dressing Italiano

    1 envelope Parmesan
      salad-dressing mix
    ¼ cup water
    2 tablespoons vinegar
    ⅔ cup mayonnaise or salad dressing
    2 teaspoons anchovy paste

Shake salad-dressing mix with water in a covered jar. Add vinegar, mayonnaise, and anchovy paste; shake to blend. Serve with Relish Salad. Makes 1 cup dressing.

Hawaiian Lemonade

A sparkling triple-fruit combination that's as refreshing as an island breeze—

    1 6-ounce can frozen
      lemonade concentrate
    1 12-ounce can (1½ cups) apricot
      nectar, chilled
    1 12-ounce can (1½ cups) unsweetened
      pineapple juice, chilled
    2 7-ounce bottles (about 2 cups)
      ginger ale, chilled

Empty lemonade concentrate into cold vacuum jug and add 1 can water; mix in fruit juices. Add ginger ale* and ice cubes; seal jug tightly. Makes 8 servings.

*Or, for more fizz, carry ginger ale in ice chest, and add just before serving.

Spread-out-and-serve basket lunches

Chilled Fruit Toddy

Add water to one 6-ounce can frozen tangerine concentrate according to label directions. Stir in one 11-ounce can (1½ cups) pear nectar, chilled, and 1 teaspoon aromatic bitters (or more to taste).

To serve, pour toddy over ice cubes. Makes ten ½-cup servings.

It's different—a formal picnic

← Curtain going up on a delightful theater party—proof that picnics can dress to fit the occasion. Roast Chicken adds a bit of elegance—flares add a touch of atmosphere.

Roast Chicken

Rinse a 3- to 4-pound ready-to-cook broiler-fryer; pat dry with paper towels. Sprinkle cavity with 1 teaspoon salt. For flavor, tuck in some celery leaves and chopped onion if you like. Push ends of drumsticks under strip of skin, if present, or tie to tail. Fold neck skin over back, fasten with skewer. Fold wings across back; tie tips together with cord.

Place breast up on rack in shallow roasting pan (or breast down, if using V-rack). Brush with melted butter or margarine. Roast uncovered in hot oven (400°) 1½ to 2¼ hours or till chicken is tender, basting occasionally with drippings.

When bird is ⅔ done, snip strip of skin or cord. (If roasted breast down, turn breast up to brown.) Continue roasting till done—thickest part of thigh meat will feel very soft when pressed between fingers (protect fingers with paper towels) and drumstick will move up and down easily. For picnic, cool chicken slightly, then chill promptly. Makes 4 servings.

Curried Picnic Salad

6 cups diced cooked potatoes
¼ cup chopped green onions and tops
2 tablespoons lemon juice
1 teaspoon celery seed
1½ teaspoons salt
½ teaspoon pepper
4 hard-cooked eggs
1 teaspoon curry powder
1 cup dairy sour cream
½ cup mayonnaise or salad dressing
2 teaspoons lemon juice
1 6-ounce jar marinated artichoke
  hearts*, drained

Combine first 6 ingredients. Separate whites and yolks of hard-cooked eggs; chop whites and add to potato mixture. Toss mixture lightly and chill.

Mash 2 of the yolks; blend in curry powder, sour cream, mayonnaise, and 2 teaspoons lemon juice. Pour over potatoes; toss lightly. Sieve remaining yolks over top. Border with marinated artichoke hearts. Keep chilled. Makes 6 to 8 servings.

*Or cook 10-ounce package frozen artichoke hearts. Chill in Italian dressing.

Limed Pineapple-in-the-Shell

1 fresh pineapple
½ cup sugar
¼ cup lime juice

Leaving the leafy top of pineapple intact, cut a slice off the top to use as lid.

Run sharp knife around inside of shell, leaving pineapple shell about ½-inch thick. Cut fruit in wedges; remove first wedge, loosen remaining wedges at bottom with grapefruit knife; lift out. Cut fruit in chunks (discard core) and mix with the sugar and lime juice. Spoon the chunks back into shell and top with the "lid"— hold in place with a skewer.

Chill fruit for 3 to 4 hours or overnight. Makes 4 or 5 servings.

Mariner's Meal

Submarine Sandwich
Piccalilli Baked Beans
Tomato Slices   Dill Mayonnaise
Green Onions for Munching
Chocolate Chippers
Brownie Cookies
Choice of Fresh Fruit
Hot Coffee   Iced Tea with Lemon

Don't forget the picnic basket when you set sail. Pack the Mariner's Meal, or try this handy plan: Each sailor gets his own lunch box with a small vacuum bottle of something hearty like spaghetti and meat balls, a cheese sandwich, plastic bag of relishes, and fresh fruit. Pack a soft drink (super-chilled awhile in freezer) next to relishes to keep 'em crisp and cold.

Aye, this is worth stowing away

'Tis a sea-faring lunch that can come ashore → anywhere. Makings for Submarine Sandwiches are kept fresh and cold in the boat's own ice chest. Each swarthy mate slices and then layers his own fillings on big crusty rolls.

Boaters' meals

Keep 'em simple for boating. In a two-seater runabout, eating space is about the same as in the family car and individually packed meals are handiest. (Or beach the boat and eat ashore.) In a larger boat, with ample spreading-out space, the meal plan can be fancier. If you've a galley, the sky's the limit!

• Canned and dried foods are handiest when space is limited. Crackers are good substitutes for bread—pack in a covered can. And fresh fruit is an easy dessert.

• If you have room to take an ice chest or vacuum or insulated jugs, you can add pre-heated and chilled foods to your list. Re-usable canned "ice" is helpful, too.

• For cooking aboard, choose a stove (1 or 2 burners) or a portable barbecue that is safely designed for boating use.

• Frozen foods should be solidly frozen when you start out. You can use frozen foods (each wrapped to prevent dripping) to help keep other foods cold.

• Investigate freeze-dried foods, too, if you have water and cooking facilities. They take minimum space, need no cooling.

• Salad: Cabbage stays crisp the longest. Packing trick: Fit a small watertight container into a larger one. Weight down inner container and fill outer one with water; freeze. When you're leaving, fill inner container with shredded cabbage. Cover. Carry oil-vinegar dressing in jar.

• Snacks! Every boat should be outfitted with a can of cookies like good voyagers below, oatmeal cookies, or vanilla wafers.

• Water? Carry containers of ice cubes. Pop a cube into mouth when thirsty. When remaining supply melts, heat the water and make instant coffee, tea, or soup.

Submarine Sandwiches

Wrap individual (miniature) French loaves to carry on picnic. Take along pre-pared mustard, garlic butter and/or may-onnaise with curry powder for spreading on split loaves of bread.

In ice chest, take baked ham, Swiss cheese, tomatoes, cucumber—to be sliced at picnic; also lettuce, olives, pickles—what-have-you. Let everyone stack up his own super sandwich.

Piccalilli Baked Beans

　6 slices bacon
　⅓ cup finely chopped onion
　2 1-pound cans (4 cups) pork
　　and beans
　½ cup drained sweet-pickle relish
　2 tablespoons molasses
　½ teaspoon salt

Fry bacon till crisp; drain and crumble. Cook onion in 2 tablespoons bacon drip-pings till tender but not brown; add to beans. Add relish, molasses, salt, and ba-con. Turn into 1½-quart casserole.

Bake in moderate oven (350°) about 50 minutes. Chill. Makes 4 or 5 servings.

Brownie Cookies

　½ cup shortening
　½ cup granulated sugar
　¼ cup brown sugar
　1 egg
　1 teaspoon vanilla
　1 1-ounce square unsweetened
　　chocolate, melted
　2 tablespoons milk
　　　　• • •
　1 cup sifted all-purpose flour
　½ teaspoon salt
　½ teaspoon soda
　½ cup chopped California walnuts

Cream together shortening, sugars, egg, and vanilla till light and fluffy. Stir in chocolate and milk. Sift together dry in-gredients; stir into creamed mixture, blend-ing well. Add nuts. Drop mixture by rounded teaspoons about 2 inches apart on greased cooky sheet.

Bake in moderate oven (350°) 10 to 12 minutes or till done. Cool slightly; remove from pan. Makes about 2 dozen.

Chocolate Chippers

Cream together ½ cup butter, ½ cup granulated sugar, and ¼ cup brown sugar. Add 1 egg; beat well. Sift together 1 cup sifted all-purpose flour, ½ teaspoon soda, and ½ teaspoon salt; stir into creamed mixture, blending well. Add 1 cup semi-sweet chocolate pieces, ½ cup chopped walnuts, and 1 teaspoon vanilla.

Drop from teaspoon 2 inches apart onto greased cooky sheet. Bake at 375° for 10 to 12 minutes. Makes about 3½ dozen.

Eat lunch hobo style

Boat Picnic

Coney Islands
Coleslaw
Cupcakes   Fresh Fruit
Iced Tea

Coney Islands

Outdoor appetites? Count on 2 Coneys apiece—

12 frankfurters, heated
12 coney buns, heated
Prepared mustard
Chopped onion
1 recipe Coney Sauce

Set everything out, help-yourself style. Folks place franks in buns, smear on mustard, spoon on onion, then hot Coney Sauce. Makes 12 Coneys.

To heat franks for picnic: Preheat a wide-mouth vacuum or insulated jug by filling with boiling water; let stand few minutes. Empty; refill jug almost to top with boiling water, leaving space for franks; add lid. When your picnickers are hungry, add franks to jug; let heat in the water, with lid on, for 7 to 10 minutes. Remove franks from water with tongs.

Coney Sauce

Long jaunt or boat trip? Take cans of chili con carne instead. (Also canned franks)—

½ pound ground beef
• • •
¼ cup water
¼ cup chopped onion
1 clove garlic, minced
1 8-ounce can (1 cup) seasoned tomato sauce
½ to ¾ teaspoon chili powder
½ teaspoon monosodium glutamate
½ teaspoon salt

Brown ground beef slowly but thoroughly, breaking with a fork till fine. Add remaining ingredients; simmer uncovered 10 minutes. Makes sauce for 12 Coneys.

Back-yard Bonanza

Peanut-butter Buns
Egg-Hamwiches
Peter Rabbit Salads
Giant Sugar Cookies with Raisins
Fresh Fruit   Cold Milk
Circus Peanuts
Peppermint Sticks

When the children beg, "Can't we eat outdoors?" let them sally forth (to the yard) each shouldering a hobo lunch. In a red bandana, place two sandwiches (wrapped up) along with a plastic or paper container of Peter Rabbit-style carrot and celery sticks rolled in a lettuce leaf. For sandwich fillings, try our simple flavor combinations given in the recipes. In each lunch, include a Giant Sugar Cooky and an orange or banana. Tie opposite corners of bandana, and run one end of the stick through the knot.

Peanut-butter Buns

Kids will clap hands for this one—

1 medium fully ripe banana
½ cup peanut butter
1 tablespoon lemon juice
Butter
Parkerhouse rolls or hamburger buns

Mash banana. Add peanut butter and lemon juice. Spread butter on rolls or buns, top with filling. Makes 1 cup filling.

Applesauce variation: Omit banana and lemon juice; add ½ cup applesauce.

Egg-Hamwiches

Easy-on-Mom sandwiches, just open a can of deviled ham and chop an egg—

1 hard-cooked egg, chopped
1 2¼-ounce can (¼ cup) deviled ham
2 tablespoons drained pickle relish

• • •

6 slices whole-wheat bread, buttered
Lettuce

Combine chopped egg, deviled ham, and pickle relish. Spread on 3 slices of bread. Top with crisp lettuce and second slice of bread. Makes 3 sandwiches.

Giant Sugar Cookies with Raisin Polka Dots

Dot raisins atop cookies at random or to make funny faces—

1 cup shortening
½ cup granulated sugar
½ cup brown sugar

• • •

2 egg yolks or 1 egg
3 tablespoons milk
2 teaspoons vanilla
2⅔ cups sifted all-purpose flour
2 teaspoons cream of tartar
1 teaspoon soda
½ teaspoon salt

• • •

Raisins

Thoroughly cream shortening and sugars. Add egg yolks, milk, and vanilla; beat well. Sift together dry ingredients; add to creamed mixture. Chill dough 1 hour.

On well-floured pastry cloth, roll the dough to ⅛ inch. Cut with a 4-inch round cutter (or use canister lid). Place several raisins atop each cooky, and sprinkle with granulated sugar.

Bake 1 inch apart on ungreased cooky sheet in moderate oven (350°) 6 to 8 minutes. Makes about 3½ dozen cookies.

The hobos meet for lunch

← Eating outdoors is a picnic — even in your own back yard! The kids vote it always more fun — no worries about crumbs or forks or fancy manners. Finger food is easy to eat.

Index

A-B

Appetizers
  Appetizer Ham Kabobs, 37
  Bacon-Cheese Bites, 36
  Broiled Banana, 37
  Cocktail Totems, 37
  Mushroom Buttons, 36
  Olives-in-Bacon, 36
  Pepper Pups, 37
  Shrimpkin, 37
  Western Starter, 36
Beans
  Barbecue Bean Salad, 32
  Beanpot, 30
  El Paso, 16
  Piccalilli Baked, 58
  Pink Beans Supreme, 30
  Saucy Baked, 40
  Skillet Beans 'n Franks, 17
Beef, see Meats
Beverages
  Chilled Fruit Toddy, 55
  Hawaiian Lemonade, 53
  Hilo Punch, 45
Breads
  Banana Bread, 45
  Barbecue Bread, 32
  Cheese Wedges, 47
  French Bread with
    Bar-B-Q Butter, 32
  Grilled Garlic Slices, 32
  Mexican Swirls, 47
  Parsley-butter Loaf, 48
  Rolls on a Spit, 32
  Texas Trail Cakes, 32
Butter, Herb, 21
Butter, Lemon, 27

C-D

Chicken
  Chicken Broilercue, 18
  Flying Drumsticks, 18
  Gourmet Marinated, 18
  Hawaiian Chicken Salad, 45
  Perfect Fried, 49
  Roast, 56
  Whirlibird Chickens, 18
Coleslaw
  Spring Coleslaw, 32
  Summer Slaw, 40
Cookies
  Brownie, 58
  Chocolate Chippers, 58
  Giant Sugar, 61
Corn, 28, 49
Cornish Capons,
  Tangerine, 19
Cornish Hens, Luscious, 19
Desserts
  Fruit
    Fruit-bobs, 33
    Ginger Peachy, 40
    Hot Banana
      Shortcake, 34
    Limed Pineapple-in-
      the-Shell, 56
    Melon-ball Refresher, 35
    Melon-patch Treats, 34
    Peach Shortcake
      Dessert Cups, 49
    Pears a la Compote, 42
    Pineapple-on-a-Spit, 33
    Ruby Fruit Compote, 42
  Grill-baked Pudding
    Cake, 35

Desserts, continued
  Hickory Nuts, 33
  Ice cream and sundaes
    Ice cream desserts, 35
    Powwow Sundae, 34
    Strawberry Ice Cream, 34
    Tropical Sundaes, 47
  Kabob
    Cake Kabobs, 33
    Candy-Cooky Poles, 33
    Cart-wheel Bananas, 33
    Donut Holes, 33
    Fruit-bobs, 33
    Roll-'n-fruit
      Dessert Bobs, 35
  Kona Coffee Torte, 45
  Lemon Angel Frost, 47
  S'mores, 34
  Strawberry Parfait Pie, 43
Deviled Eggs, 41

F-G-H

Filling, Orange, 45
Fish and sea food
  Bacon-stuffed Trout, 20
  Fillets with Caper
    Sauce, 20
  Fish and Bacon, 20
  Fish in Corn Husks, 20
  Herbed Fish Grill, 20
  Sea-food Sword, 27
  Shore Dinner on Kabob, 27
  Shrimpkin, 37
  Tuna Mousse, 47
Frankfurters
  Circle Pups, 9
  Cocktail Totems, 37
  Coney Islands, 59
  Dunking Frankfurters, 8
  Frank Wrap-ups, 9
  Hilo Franks, 8
  Hot Dogie-burgers, 11
  Nutty Pups, 9
  Pepper Pups, 37
  Pig-in-a-Poke, 25
  Rafted Wieners, 9
  Skillet Beans 'n
    Franks, 17
  Sloppy Joe Franks, 8
Frosting, Mocha, 45
Glaze, Ginger, 24
Grill tips, 11
Ham, 22, 23, 37
Hamburgers
  Aloha Burgers, 10
  Burgundy Beef burgers, 11
  Favorite Grilled, 11
  Giant Burgers, 11
  Hot Dogie-burgers, 11
  Mountain Burgers, 10
  Pennyburgers, 11
  Two-faced, 13
  Whopper-burgers, 13
Hickory smoking, 19

K-L-M

Kabobs, 25-27, 35-37
Lamb
  Armenian Shish Kebab, 26
  Chili Grill-roasted, 22
  Marinated Lamb
    Squares, 25
  Orange-stuffed Leg of, 21
  Saucy Lamb Riblets, 16
Meats, see also Poultry
  Beef
    Chef's Chuck Roast, 14
    Island Teriyaki, 17
    Kettle Barbecued Pot
      Roast, 16
    Marinated Beef Cubes, 25
    Mexican Beef Kabobs, 26
    On-a-Saber Beef, 26

Meats, Beef, continued
    Roast Beef with Herb
      Butter, 21
    Roast, Rotisserie, 21
  Steak
    Cracked-pepper, 16
    Grilled Steaks, 23
    In-a-minute Steaks, 52
    Swank Porterhouse, 23
  Bologna, Barbecued, 17
  Frankfurters
    Circle Pups, 9
    Dunking Frankfurters, 8
    Frank Wrap-ups, 9
    Hilo Franks, 8
    Hot Dogie-burgers, 11
    Nutty Pups, 9
    Pig-in-a-Poke, 25
    Rafted Wieners, 9
    Sloppy Joe Franks, 8
  Hamburgers
    Aloha Burgers, 10
    Burgundy Beefburgers, 11
    Favorite Grilled, 11
    Giant Burgers, 11
    Hot Dogie-burgers, 11
    Mountain Burgers, 10
    Pennyburgers, 11
    Two-faced, 13
    Whopper-burgers, 13
  Lamb
    Armenian Shish
      Kebab, 26
    Chili Grill-roasted, 22
    Marinated Lamb
      Squares, 25
    Orange-stuffed Leg of, 21
    Roast, Rotisserie, 21
    Saucy Lamb Riblets, 16
  Lunch-on-a-Stick, 25
  Luncheon Meat, Cheese-
    frosted, 17
  Mandarin Dinner, 25
  Patio Fiesta Dinner, 15
  Pork
    Abacus Ribs, 26
    Barbecue-glazed Ham, 23
    On-the-grill Spareribs, 24
    Orange-glazed Ham 'n
      Pineapple, 23
    Peanut-buttered Pork
      Roast, 21
    Roast Pork Chops, 24
    Roast, Rotisserie, 21
    Spinning Ham, 22
    Spit-barbecued Ribs, 24
  Stew, Camp, 15
Melons, 32, 34-35

P

Picnics, 52-61
Pork, see Meats
Potato Salads, 31, 41, 56
Potatoes, 29, 30, 49
Poultry
  Chicken, 18, 49, 56
  Cornish Capons,
    Tangerine, 19
  Cornish Hens, Luscious, 19
  Turkey, Hickory
    Smoked, 19
  Turkey, Rotisserie, 19
Punch, Hilo, 45

R-S-T

Relishes
  Gosh and Golly Relish, 37
  Hot Chop-Chop, 37
  Red Onion Relish, 30
Ribs, 24, 26
Rice, Barbecued, 29
Roasts, 14, 16, 21
Salad dressings

Clear French Dressing, 31
Horseradish Dressing, 31
Olive Dressing, 52
Orange Dressing, 31
Parmesan Dressing
  Italiano, 53
Salads
  Barbecue Bean Salad, 32
  Calico Potato Salad, 31
  Curried Picnic Salad, 56
  Fruited Melon Cups, 32
  Garden Perfection Loaf, 46
  Hawaiian Chicken Salad, 45
  Little Caesar Salad, 31
  Perfection Salad, 46
  Potluck Potato Salad, 31
  Relish Salad, 53
  Sour-cream Potato
    Salad, 41
  Spring Coleslaw, 32
  Summer Slaw, 40
  Tomato Salad Mold, 49
  Tuna Mousse, 47
Sandwiches
  Bacon 'n Tomato Special, 43
  Big Beef Sandwich, 15
  Coney Islands, 59
  Egg-Hamwiches, 61
  Lattice Cheese, 43
  Peanut-butter Buns, 59
  Spicy Pork, 17
  Steak, 16
  Submarine, 58
  Walking Sandwich, 40
Sauce
  Caper, 20
  Coney, 59
  Quick Bordelaise, 14
  Real-hot, 24
  Tartare, 27
Sea food, see Fish
Soups
  Easy Vichyssoise, 42
  Jellied Consomme, 42
  Tomato Cooler, 42
Steak, see Meats
Stews, 15
Teriyaki, Island, 17
Trout, Bacon-stuffed, 20
Tuna Mousse, 47
Turkey, 19

V

Vegetables, Rice
  Beans
    Beanpot, 30
    Piccalilli Baked, 58
    Pink Beans Supreme, 30
    Saucy Baked, 40
  Corn
    Anise, 28
    Bacon Ears, 28
    Corn Coblets, 49
    Hickory-barbecued
      Ears, 28
    Roasted Ears, 28
  Potatoes
    Foiled Potatoes with
      Parmesan, 30
    Foiled Spuds, 29
    Onioned, 29
    Potato Patties, 49
    Skillet, 29
  Rice, Barbecued, 29
  Tomatoes
    Grill-top, 29
    Herbed, 42
    Tomatoes in Foil, 28
  Vegetables, Foiled, 28
  Vegetables on a Spit, 29

Photographs, Creative Cooking
Library: Allen Snook, Wesley
Bowman.